Director
REGISTERS and RECORDS

Customs e Excise.
Advice Centre.
London Central.
020 7865 4400

Directory of
REGISTERS and
RECORDS

Bryan Abraham

Consulting Editor
Trevor M Aldridge
QC(Hon) MA(Cantab), Solicitor

FIFTH EDITION

© Longman Group UK Ltd 1993

ISBN 0 75200 0012

First published 1963
Revised and reprinted 1964
Second edition 1966
Third edition 1976
Fourth edition 1984
Fifth edition 1993

Published by
Longman Law, Tax and Finance
Longman Group UK Ltd
21–27 Lamb's Conduit Street
London WC1N 3NJ

Associated Offices
Australia, Hong Kong, Malaysia, Singapore, USA

A CIP catalogue record for this book is available from the British Library.

Printed and bound in Great Britain by
Biddles Ltd, Guildford and King's Lynn

Preface

A great deal of factual information is available from official and similar public records. Fast and efficient access to it can be a considerable help in legal practice, as well as in other contexts. This book aims to help those who need information in two ways. First, it draws attention to sources which will be unfamiliar to some. Secondly, it gives practical details which all enquirers will need: addresses, telephone numbers, fees and opening hours.

This edition has again been thoroughly revised and updated. A lot more information has been added, indeed there are well over twenty new sections. Some of these give more details about registers in other parts of the British Isles, both for personal and commercial information. There are also new registers, notably of data users and bureaux (Data Protection Act 1984), the Securities and Investments Board's Central Register (Financial Services Act 1986), and those established by the organisations privatised since the last edition (Oftel, Ofgas, Offer, etc). The increasing importance of county record offices in storing older records which can still be of practical importance is recognised by a list of their addresses in the Appendix.

Once again, officials of many of the offices mentioned have generously given invaluable help. This has undoubtedly increased the accuracy of the information, although it does not imply any official recognition. The details for this edition were collected during spring 1993, and while they were understood to be correct when the book went to press, readers must take into account possible changes, particularly in fees, since then.

However hard it tries, a book like this cannot be truly comprehensive. Comments from any reader who cares to write with any suggestion of other sources of information which it would be useful to include will be received with gratitude.

1 May 1993

Contents

Personal

Births, marriages and deaths

England and Wales

Information available

General registers of births, marriages and deaths in England and Wales (and certain others) are kept by the Registrar General. Information is available by bespeaking copy certificates, which normally give the following details:

Birth certificates Date and place of birth, sex and names of child (and names added later on baptism or otherwise), names of mother (including maiden name) and father, their places of birth (on registrations after 31 March 1969), father's occupation, and name and capacity of informant. Short birth certificates omit references to parents.

Marriage certificates Date and place of marriage, names, ages, marital status and occupations of the parties.

Death certificates Date, place and cause of death, name and home address of the deceased (on registrations after 31 March 1969), the deceased's date and place of birth and maiden name where a married woman. The name and capacity of the informant is also given in every case.

Registrations for the main records of births, marriages and deaths in England and Wales started on 1 July 1837. Records of births and deaths at sea (the Marine Register Book), which relate chiefly to English and Welsh persons, also date from then. Registration in the Air Register Book is of births and deaths on, and persons missing from, aircraft registered in Great Britain and Northern

Ireland occurring anywhere in the world started in 1949, and in respect of hovercraft since 1 November 1972. There are records of deaths on or from certain offshore installations from 30 November 1972.

Service records of births, marriages and deaths occurring outside the United Kingdom among members of the armed forces and their families also include certain other persons connected or working with the services, or occurring on board certain ships and aircraft used for service purposes. The Army registers date mainly from 1881, but some entries extend back to 1761. RAF returns started in 1920. Full returns for the Royal Navy only started in 1959; prior to that only occurrences actually on board HM ships (and recorded in the ships' logs) were registered. The registers include presumed deaths.

Births, marriages and deaths of British subjects in foreign countries are registered by consular officers, and the register of their returns dates from July 1849. Returns from some British High Commissioners for the more recently independent Commonwealth countries relating to United Kingdom citizens and certain other British nationals are also maintained. The Registrar General has some miscellaneous records of births, baptisms, marriages, deaths and burials, including some foreign marriage documents where at least one party was British. (See also Parish Registers, p 9 and Pedigrees, p 34.)

A register of still-births in England and Wales since 1 July 1927 is also maintained. It shows the date and place, parents' names, addresses and (since 1 April 1969) place of birth, father's occupation, sex of baby and cause of still-birth.

A register of births of abandoned children has been maintained since 1 January 1977. Entries show the child's date and place of birth, name, surname and sex. No details of parentage are recorded, and only short birth certificates are issued.

The dates of birth, and where appropriate death, of many well-known people are recorded in *Who's Who* and *Who Was Who* (A & C Black Ltd).

To whom available

Anyone may obtain certificates, except in the case of the records of still-births, where the express permission of the Registrar General is required, and this is usually given only where the certificate is required for production in court.

How obtained

Certificates may be obtained by personal attendance or by post from:

> *Personal attendance* The Registrar General, General Register Office, St Catherines House, 10 Kingsway, London WC2B 6JP (Tel: 071–242 0262).

> *Post* General Register Office, Postal Applications Section, Smedley Hydro, Trafalgar Road, Southport, Merseyside PR8 2HH (Tel: 0704 63563).

The search rooms are open Monday–Friday, 8.30 am to 4.30 pm, save for the first Tuesday in each month when they open at 10 am.

Indexes are available to the main records of events in England and Wales. They are made up alphabetically by quarters, with separate ones for births, marriages and deaths. They give references which enable the staff to locate the certified copies of entries, which are not available for public inspection. These indexes are available between nine and 12 months after the close of the quarter to which they relate. The certificate is usually available after two days. Copy certificates may always be obtained from the local superintendent registrar in whose district the actual registration was made. After his returns have been made to St Catherines House, but before the indexes are completed, a search can sometimes be carried out by the staff at St Catherines House among the records waiting to be indexed if precise details are known. In the latter case a search fee is payable in respect of each registration district searched. Certificates from returns from consular offices and British High Commissioners are available from the Registrar General about six months after the end of the year in which the registration is made.

Postal applications are made by letter and should give the fullest particulars known: at least the date and place of the event and full name(s). The certificate is posted after approximately three weeks.

Cost

Certificates on personal application are £5.50 each, except short birth certificates, £3.50. Certificates, by post, £15 or £13 respectively (£3 retained if search unsuccessful). If 'reference information' (ie quarter or year of event, and volume number, page number and district from the OPCS index) is supplied, the cost is £3 less. Certificates are issued by local registrars at reduced rates for the purposes of certain Acts, namely: Social Security, National Insurance, National Insurance (Industrial Injuries), Education, Young Persons (Employment), Shops, Factories, Friendly Societies, Industrial Injuries (old cases); and for purposes of the National and Trustee Savings Banks, War or National Savings Certificates, savings contracts, Premium Savings Bonds and Government Annuities.

Admissibility in evidence

A certified copy entry relating to birth, marriage or death in England or Wales, under the seal of the General Register Office, is admissible in evidence (Marriage Act 1949, s 65(3); Births and Deaths Registration Act 1953, s 34(6)). Certain restrictions apply to other register entries in cases of delayed registration and certain other irregularities. Certified copies of entries in the service department registers are also admissible (Registration of Births, Deaths and Marriages (Special Provisions) Act 1957, s 3(2)).

Authenticated copies from certain overseas public registers are admissible in evidence. Orders under the Oaths and Evidence (Overseas Authorities and Countries) Act 1963, have been made in respect of the following countries: Denmark (Evidence (Denmark) Order 1969), Ireland (Evidence (Republic of Ireland) Order 1969), Italy (Evidence (Italy) Order 1969), United States (evidence (United States of America) Order 1969), and West Germany including West Berlin (Evidence (Federal Republic of Germany) Order 1970). A series of orders has been made under the Evidence (Foreign Dominion and Colonial Documents) Act 1933, relating to countries and territories now or formerly within the Commonwealth.

Scotland

Information available

The information available from the registers in Scotland is similar to that from those in England and Wales, although the dates on which registrations started often vary. The main registers of births, marriages and deaths started on 1 January 1855. There is also a register of neglected entries, recording births, marriages and deaths proved to have occurred in Scotland between 1801 and 1854, but not entered in the parish registers. The register of still-births was started in 1939.

Registers of births, marriages and deaths outside Scotland include: marine register of births and deaths on British registered merchant ships from 1855; air register of births and deaths in aircraft registered in the UK from 1948; army returns from military stations abroad 1881 to 1959; service department registers from 1 April 1959 which include not only service personnel but their families; marriages solemnised by army chaplains outside the UK since 1892; war registers of deaths in the Boer War, World War I (not officers) and World War II (incomplete); consular returns, of births and deaths since 1914, and marriages since 1917; high commissioners' returns from 1964 (not complete). There is a register from 1860 to 1965 of births, deaths and marriages in foreign countries, compiled from information supplied by the parties, and copies of certificates (with translations) of some foreign marriages when no British consul was present.

To whom available

Anyone may search, except that details from the register of still-births are only made available in exceptional circumstances, eg for legal proceedings.

How obtained

Application may be made personally or by post to:

General Register Office for Scotland, New Register House, Edinburgh EH1 3YT (Tel: 031–334 0380).

Cost

All certificates: £8.50 on personal application, £11.50 by post.

Admissibility in evidence

A certified copy entry relating to a birth, marriage or death in Scotland, under the seal of the General Register Office in Edinburgh, is admissible in evidence (Registration of Births, Deaths and Marriages (Scotland) Acts 1854 to 1938).

Northern Ireland

Information available

The contents of certificates in Northern Ireland are generally the same as those of registrations in England and Wales. Records of births and deaths started on 1 January 1864. The civil registration of marriages, other than Roman Catholic marriages, started on 1 April 1845. This was extended to Roman Catholic marriages on 1 January 1864. The records relating to marriages are only held centrally in Belfast for marriages from 1922 onwards. Earlier records are held by district registrars, whose addresses can be obtained from the General Registrar Office. For information prior to 31 December 1921, see also under Republic of Ireland (p 7 below).

To whom available

Anyone may search.

How obtained

Certificates may be obtained by personal attendance or post from:

General Register Office, Oxford House, 49–55 Chichester St, Belfast BT1 4HF (Tel: 0232 235211).

Cost

Full birth, marriage or death certificate, £5.50 (if full details including register number supplied, £3.50). Short birth certificate, £3.50. Searches, £2 for each period of five years (the first five-year fee is included in the certificate cost), or £5 for general search for up to six hours.

Admissibility in evidence

Authenticated copies of certificates are admissible in evidence: Ireland (Registration of Births and Deaths) (Ireland) Act 1863, s 5; Births and Deaths Registration (Ireland) Act 1880, s 28; Marriages (Ireland) Act 1844, s 71; Marriage Law (Ireland) Amendments Acts 1863 and 1873; Matrimonial Causes and Marriage Law (Ireland) Amendments Act 1870.

Republic of Ireland

Information available

The contents of birth, marriage and death certificates in the Republic of Ireland are substantially the same as in those issued in England and Wales. Since 1 January 1956, marriage certificates include an entry 'intended future permanent residence'. Registers of births and deaths are held for the whole of Ireland from 1 January 1864 to 31 December 1921, and after then for the Republic only. The registers of marriages from 1 April 1845 to 31 December 1863 relate to marriages throughout Ireland, other than those celebrated by the Roman Catholic clergy. From 1 January 1864 all marriages are registered, but from 1 January 1922 the records relate only to the Republic. There are also records of marriages celebrated by the Minister of the German Protestant Church, Dublin, from 1806 to 1837 (incl).

Other registers include: births of children of Irish parents and deaths of Irish born persons certified by British consuls 1 January 1864 to 31 December 1921; births at sea of children with one Irish parent and deaths at sea of Irish persons, from 1 January 1864, excluding Northern Ireland after 31 December 1921; certain occurrences in the services; certain births and deaths outside the Republic; and certain Lourdes marriages.

To whom available

Anyone may search.

How obtained

Application may be made in person or by post to:

Oifig an Ard-Chlaraitheora, Joyce House, 8–11 Lombard Street East, Dublin 2 (Tel: 010 353 1 711000). The office is open Monday–Friday, 9.30 am to 12.30 pm, 2.15 pm to 4.30 pm.

Cost

Certificates including search fee, full £5.50, short birth certificate £3.50. Searches, £1.50 per five-year period (the first being included in the certificate fee), or £12 for six hours.

Admissibility in evidence

See under Northern Ireland, p 7 above.

Jersey

Information available

The registers of births, marriages and deaths contain similar information to that shown for England and Wales. The records were started in August 1842. Some earlier records do exist. They are held by the rectors and vicars of the parishes.

To whom available

Anyone may search.

How obtained

Applications should be made by post—there are no personal searching facilities—to:

The Superintendent Registrar, States' Office, Royal Square, St Helier, Jersey (Tel: 0534 502335).

If the event is known to have occurred in St Helier, application may be made to:

The Registrar, Town Hall, York Street, St Helier, Jersey.

Cost

Search, £5 per five-year period. Full certificate, £5, short birth certificate, £1.

Parish registers

Information available

Parish registers record burials, marriages and baptisms. Some are extant for a considerable period, possibly to as early as 1538. The contents of the records vary.

Scottish parish registers from 1553–1854, when compulsory civil registration of births, marriages and deaths started there, have been collected and deposited in the General Register Office. They are not complete, and the contents vary. Only a few of the 4,000 volumes are indexed.

To whom available

Anyone may search. At the Public Record Office, a reader's ticket is required.

How obtained

Many records have now been transferred to diocesan record offices, or county record offices designated as such by the bishop. Enquiry is best first made of the county record office. Where records are still in the custody of the parish, enquiry should be made of the incumbent.

The National Register of Archives is a central collection point for information about the nature and location of historical records, including those of Anglican parishes and Roman Catholic and non-conformist churches.

It is kept by:

> The Historical Manuscripts Commissioner, Quality House, Quality Court, Chancery Lane, London WC2A 1HP (Tel: 071–242 1198).

The search room is open Monday–Friday, 9.30 am to 5 pm. Only limited and specific enquiries can be answered by post.

Many non-conformist registers have been transferred in bulk to the Public Record Office, after being sent to the Registrar General for authentication or safe custody under the Non-Parochial Register Act 1840 and the Births and Deaths Registration Act 1858. Personal application to inspect them should be made to:

> Public Record Office, Chancery Lane, London WC2A 1LR (Tel: 081–876 3444 – this number covers the Public Record Offices at Kew and Chancery Lane).

Many other non-conformist registers are deposited in county record offices or retained locally.

Applications relating to Scottish records should be made in person or by post to:

> General Register Office for Scotland, New Register House, Edinburgh EH1 3YT (Tel: 031–334 0380).

The search room is open Monday–Friday, 9.00 am to 4.30 pm (4 pm on Fridays).

Cost

No fee is charged by the Commission, the Public Record Office and most county record offices.

Fees to Church of England incumbents: search of pre-1837 marriage records, first hour £7, each subsequent hour £5; baptismal and burial records, first hour's search (including copy of one entry) £7, each subsequent hour £5, additional copies £7 each.

Scottish records: fee for extract if sufficient identifying information supplied £6 for official extract, £2 for photocopy; general search by enquirer, £15 per day.

Admissibility in evidence

Parish registers are admissible in evidence on production from proper custody (Parochial Registers Act 1812). A copy or extract signed and certified by the person having custody of the original is equally admissible (Evidence Act 1851). Short certificates of baptism are treated similarly (Baptismal Registers Measure 1961, s 2(2)).

Adoptions

England and Wales

Information available

Certificates may be obtained from the Registrar General of any adoption in England and Wales since 1 January 1927. They show date and court of adoption, name of child as adopted, and full names and address of adoptive parents. A separate index is maintained which connects each entry in the Adopted Children Register to the entry in the Births Register relating to the same child.

To whom available

Anyone may obtain certificates from the Adopted Children Register. Entries from the index connecting it with the Births Register will only be disclosed upon the authority of an order of the High Court, the Westminster County Court, or the court which made the original adoption order.

A person who has been adopted and who has attained the age of 18 may obtain a copy of his birth certificate. The applicant must first attend for an interview with a counsellor. Someone who has been adopted and who is intending to be married can obtain a statement from the Registrar General as to whether or not it appears from his register that the parties to the proposed marriage are within the prohibited degrees of relationship.

How obtained

Certificates from the Adopted Children Register are obtained by post from:

General Register Office, Postal Applications Section, Smedley Hydro, Trafalgar Road, Southport, Merseyside PR8 2HH (Tel: 051–471 4831).

Or by personal application to:

General Register Office, St Catherines House, 10 Kingsway, London WC2B 6JP (Tel:071–242 0262).

Cost

Certificates from the Adopted Children Register, on personal application: £5.50 or £3.50 in short form omitting details of parents; by post: £12 or £10 in the short form (£6 retained if search unsuccessful).

Admissibility in evidence

A certified copy entry under the seal of the General Register Office is admissible in evidence (Adoption Act 1958, s 20(2)).

Scotland

Information available

The register of adoptions under orders made by the Scottish courts starts in 1930. No entries relate to persons born before October 1909.

To whom available

Anyone may search.

How obtained

Personal or postal application should be made to:

General Register Office for Scotland, New Register House, Edinburgh EH1 3YT (Tel: 031–334 0380).

Cost

Certificates: by post, full or short £11.50; personal application, full or short £8.50.

Republic of Ireland

Information available

Details of adoptions in the Irish Republic are available from 10 July 1953.

To whom available

Anyone may search.

How obtained

Personal or postal application should be made to:

Oifig an Ard-Chlaraitheora, Joyce House, 8–11 Lombard Street East, Dublin 2 (Tel: 010 353 1 711000).

Cost

Certificates, full £5.50, short £3.50.

Human fertilisation and embryology

Information available

Whether treatment services have been provided to any identifiable individual, whether the gametes of any such individual have been kept or used or whether an embryo has been taken from an identifiable woman, and whether any identifiable individual was or may have been born as a result of such treatment services. (In this connection, 'treatment services' includes insemination by donor (ID) and *in vitro* fertilisation (IVF).)

To whom available

The public may not apply. The information is available only to persons over eighteen, who have a right to ascertain genetic information relating to their genetic parent, or whether persons who propose to marry are or might be related. In addition, a person under eighteen who proposes to marry may ascertain whether he or she is or may be related to the intended spouse, provided that it can be shown that the person in question was or may have been born as a result of treatment services *and* that he or she has had a suitable opportunity to receive proper counselling about the implications of the request.

How obtained

Application should be made, by post, to:

> The Human Fertilisation and Embryology Authority, Paxton House, 30 Artillery Lane, London E1 7LS (Tel: 071–377 5077; Fax: 071–377 1871).

Note, however, that this register has been in effect only since 1 August 1990. It follows therefore that the earliest anyone may apply will be in 2006.

Changes of name

By deed poll

Information available

When a change of name is evidenced by a deed poll which is enrolled at the Central Office of the Supreme Court (which by no means all deeds poll are), the enrolled copy may be inspected and copies obtained. The records are sent to the Public Record Office three years after enrolment. Deeds poll may also be registered at the College of Arms (see below under By Royal Licence).

In Scotland, changes of name are commonly recorded in the registers of the court of the Lord Lyon. Applications for information should be addressed to:

> The Lyon Clerk and Keeper of the Records, Court of the Lord Lyon, New Register House, Edinburgh EH1 3YT (Tel: 031–334 0380).

To whom available

Anyone may search.

How obtained

Application should be made in person to:

> Room E07, Royal Courts of Justice, Strand, London WC2A 2LL, or

Public Record Office, Chancery Lane, London WC2A 1LR
(Tel: 081-876 3444).

Cost

Central Office, search fee £1 per hour or part. Copies: up to
foolscap size, 25p (photographic), 50p (typed), per sheet. Public
Record Office, no search fee. Copies: cost depends on size and
method of reproduction.

Admissibility in evidence

Office copies of deeds filed at the Central Office are admissible
in evidence (RSC, Ord 38, r 10). Certified copies under the seal
of the Public Record Office of deeds filed there are similarly
admissible (Public Records Act 1958, s 9).

By royal licence

Information available

All changes of name authorised by royal licence are recorded
at the College of Arms. A transcription of the records may be
obtained.

To whom available

Anyone may enquire.

How obtained

Enquiries should be made by letter to:

College of Arms, Queen Victoria Street, London EC4V 4BT
(Tel: 071-236 7728).

Cost

The charge varies according to the work entailed.

By Act of Parliament

Information available

An additional way to change a name formerly used was by private
Act of Parliament. For the period 1845 to 1859, these private Acts

are included in the officially printed series of Acts. For other periods, the unpublished original Acts in Parliament are the official record.

To whom available

Anyone may search.

How obtained

Application must be made to:

> The Clerk of the Records, House of Lords Record Office, House of Lords, London SW1A 0PW (Tel: 071–219 3074).

Older changes generally

Information available

Many changes of name are recorded in *An Index to Change of Name 1760–1901*, ed, W P W Phillimore and E A Fry (1905), a copy of which is available in the Public Record Office. This draws together name changes recorded in private Acts of Parliament, royal licences published in the *London Gazette* and the *Dublin Gazette*, notices published in *The Times* after 1861, some from other newspapers, the register of the Lord Lyon, and records in the office of the Ulster King of Arms, and some private information. Although extensive, this record is not comprehensive.

Naturalisation

There are published the full names of every person naturalised (with changes on naturalisation), and his or her address, country of origin and date of naturalisation.

Although rare after 1844, naturalisation by Act of Parliament survived until 1911. The unpublished original Acts in Parliament are the official record.

How obtained

Enquiries may be addressed to:

Home Office, Nationality Division, 3rd Floor, India Buildings, Water Street, Liverpool L2 0QN (Tel: 051-236 4723).

Application for information about Acts of Parliament should be made to:

The Clerk of the Records, House of Lords Record Office, House of Lords, London SW1A 0PW (Tel: 071-219 3074).

Divorce

Information available

Copies of decrees nisi and absolute can be obtained which show the names of the parties, the date of the decree, to whom it was granted, on what grounds and sometimes the court's decision on subsidiary matters.

To whom available

Anyone may obtain copies. Copies of decrees nisi not made absolute are available only to persons who can give the title of the case and date of the decree.

How obtained

Personal application or written is made to:

Principal Registry, Family Division, Room G27B (Divorce Registry), Somerset House, Strand, London WC2R 1LP (Tel: 071-936 6966).

Yearly indexes are kept here and copies may be bespoken. Although there are complete indexes in London, copies of decrees made in district registry cases must be bespoken at the district registry concerned. Applicants should furnish the full names of the parties and, ideally, date (or year) of marriage and final decree, and place of marriage.

Cost

Search fee, £5 for each ten-year period or part. Office copy, 25p.

Accidents

Industrial

Information available

In connection with a claim for social security (industrial injuries) benefit the employer completes a form confirming details of the accident and whether it arose out of or in connection with employed earner's employment. This form is sent to the Department of Social Security, and correspondence between the Department and the employer and the Department and the employee may ensue. The contents of the form and the correspondence are available in certain circumstances.

See also Medical Records, p 19.

To whom available

The Department will only give details to the party which originally made the statement. However, Crown privilege is not claimed so that the information can be obtained as evidence on subpœna, but in that case it will not be divulged until the documents are actually produced in the witness box.

How obtained

Application should be made to the manager of the local office of the Department of Social Security. He will on request nominate an officer to receive a subpoena duces tecum.

Cost

Unless documents are to be produced in evidence no fee is charged.

Road traffic

Information available

For all accidents of which the police take details a summary of the information collected by them can be obtained. This includes details of the site of the accident, the vehicles involved, names and addresses of drivers and witnesses, insurance particulars given by drivers, and the names of police officers who were witnesses or took details.

See also Inquests and post-mortems, p 23.

To whom available

Any interested person may obtain a copy of the report.

How obtained

Application should be made by letter to the chief officer of police for the district, identifying the incident as exactly as possible and sending the fee.

Cost

Fee for report, £44.

Medical records

National Health Service

Information available

Every person's medical history is recorded in the records kept by the general practitioner upon whose list he is for the time being. When the patient is changing doctors, and sometimes for other reasons, the records are returned to the local National Health Service Family Practitioner Committee. Hospital records on patients are retained by the hospitals, although reports of hospital examinations and treatment may be kept with the patient's general records.

To whom available

Except sometimes to the patient himself or on his authority, medical records will not usually be divulged except on, or in anticipation of, a court order. The doctor or hospital concerned will decide whether any information is to be given.

How obtained

If the location of the records is known, application should first be made to the doctor or hospital concerned. Where the family doctor's records are required, but the present whereabouts of the patient is not known, the National Health Service Central Register will be able to say under the control of which Family Practitioner Committee the records are for the time being. Contact:

National Health Service Central Register, Smedley Hydro, Southport, Merseyside PR8 2HH (Tel: 0704 69824).

Crown privilege is not claimed for National Health Service medical records.

Social security

Information available

Self certificates and doctors' certificates sent to the Department of Social Security for the purpose of obtaining benefits are kept for only a short time. Details are recorded by the Department of the exact periods of sickness and the reasons given. A certified copy of this part of the Department's records will be made available for the purposes of personal injury claims. Reports of medical boards giving clinical findings and assessing degrees of disablement are also disclosed. If no claim for statutory sick pay is made, the Department will hold no records.

How obtained

Application should be made to the manager of the local office of the Department dealing with the case, giving details of the information required and the reasons why it is necessary. When required for a civil claim for damages, copies of the medical board reports will be supplied to the patient. They will not, however, be disclosed to the defendants without the patient's consent. The originals will be produced in court on subpoena irrespective of consent. But even then, if the patient has withheld his consent, no details will be given to the defendants until the documents are actually produced in the witness box. The local manager will nominate on request an officer to receive a subpoena duces tecum.

Army

Information available

Army medical records are treated as confidential and are not disclosed except to medical advisers nominated by the patient, his legal advisers or insurers. In the normal case copies of medical records will be sent direct to the medical adviser. In a small number of cases enquiries will be answered directly by the staff of the Director General Medical Services (Army). In criminal cases, where the medical records are considered to be relevant, photostat copies will be supplied to the defence solicitors and the originals produced in court on subpoena. Medical records of a soldier's family when treated by the Army Medical Service are dealt with in the same way as those of soldiers.

How obtained

For other ranks applications should be addressed to the Record Office of the Regiment or Corps concerned. The addresses are published in the *Army List*.

For officers application should be made to:

Ministry of Defence (AODO), London Road, Stanmore, Middx HA7 4PZ

In the case of an accident treated by a military hospital, application should be made direct to the hospital. Before serving a subpoena, in order to obtain directions for service, solicitors should consult:

Ministry of Defence DS15(L2), Whitehall, London SW1A 2HB.

Royal Navy

Records are disclosed following principles similar to those stated above for the Army. Applications should be addressed to:

The Medical Director General (Naval), Ministry of Defence, First Avenue House, High Holborn, London WC1V 6HE.

Royal Air Force

At the request of the patient, his legal advisers or insurers, the Ministry of Defence (Air Force Department) is normally prepared to provide solicitors or insurers with a summary of treatment received and conditions noted in cases of accidents and pension applications. The patient's written consent is required. In criminal cases, the practice is similar to that of the Army (see above). Enquiries should be addressed to:

DDPM5 RAF Personnel Management Centre, RAF Innsworth, Glos GL3 1EZ.

Subpoenas should be served at the above address, unless they relate to records of treatment at RAF or other service hospitals. In that case the hospital itself should be contacted first.

Ex-servicemen

Medical records relating to former members of the armed forces are transferred to the Department of Social Security for permanent retention.

Social security benefits

Information available

The Department of Social Security will give details of benefits paid and for what periods, for the purposes of a claim under the Law Reform (Personal Injuries) Act 1948, s 2. The details will not include any statement as to how the amount of the benefit was calculated, but it may be possible to deduce this. Details will also be supplied to a magistrates' clerk in connection with maintenance or affiliation proceedings on his specific request, in which case a copy of the information supplied is sent to the claimant.

How obtained

Application should be made by letter to the manager of the local office of the Department which is dealing with the case. It is essential to state that a claim under the section quoted has been formulated and that that claim includes a claim for loss of earnings. It is not essential for proceedings to have been issued.

Inquests and post-mortems

Information available

All documents in the possession of the coroner in connection with inquests and post-mortems (except exhibits at inquests) are available. These include notes of evidence made by the coroner and post-mortem examination reports in non-inquest cases, but exclude reports of preliminary enquiries and police reports not in evidence. The records must be kept for fifteen years, but may be destroyed thereafter. Information may be subject to statutory restrictions on inspection, eg the Official Secrets Acts.

To whom available

Anyone who in the opinion of the coroner is a properly interested person may inspect.

How obtained

The records may be kept by the coroner (to whom application should be made first), or if he has insufficient storage space he may transfer them to the local authority.

Cost

Inspection, free. Photocopies of documents, 80p per page.

Service records

Army

Information available

The full service records are available in certain circumstances. Leave is not always recorded on the permanent Army Department records, which are therefore not always reliable on this point. Records of pay are destroyed as a matter of routine after seven years. As to Medical Records, see p 21; as to Addresses, see p 31.

To whom available

Particulars will be supplied to the soldier's solicitor, but in the absence of a subpoena to no one else without the soldier's authority, or, if dead, that of his next-of-kin. Records at the Public Record Office (see next paragraph) are open without restriction.

How obtained

Initial enquiries in respect of all serving and former order ranks should be addressed to the Record Office of the Regiment or Corps concerned, at the address shown in the *Army List*. Application should be made to:

Serving and reserve officers   Ministry of Defence (AODO), London Rd, Stanmore, Middx HA7 4PZ.

Ex-officers   Army Records Centre, Hayes, Middx.

Ranks discharged before 1900   Public Record Office, Chancery Lane, London WC2A 1LR (Tel: 081–876 3444).

A few days' notice may be required for inspection. Some very old records relating to officers are also held by the Public Record Office.

Royal Navy

Restrictions upon the production of records are similar to those imposed by the Army (see above). Records of service, pay, pensions and leave should be applied for as follows—

Officers (records of service)   The Naval Secretary, Ministry of Defence, Old Admiralty Building, Spring Gardens, London SW1A 2BE.

Officers (pay and pensions) and ratings (pay)   The Commodore, HMS Centurion, Grange Road, Gosport, Hants PO13 9XA.

RN and WRNS ratings (pensions)   DGDA Accounts 1A1, Whittington Road, Worcester WR5 2LA.

RM other ranks   Director of Drafting and Records Royal Marines, HMS Centurion, Grange Road, Gosport, Hants PO13 9XA.

In maintenance and affiliation cases, and whenever information is required for legal proceedings, enquiries should first be addressed to:

Naval Law Division, Ministry of Defence, Old Admiralty Building, Spring Gardens, London SW1A 2BE.

The purpose of the enquiry should always be stated.

See also Medical Records, p 22; Addresses, p 32.

Royal Air Force

The Ministry of Defence (Air Force Department) holds officers' records of service permanently. Airmen's personal documents are generally destroyed five years after discharge or termination of reserve liability. Details of periods for which different classes of documents are kept are given in *Queen's Regulations for the Royal Air Force*, Appendix 3, s 2 (HMSO). Certain records of service are retained permanently at the RAF Record Office, and these will normally suffice to answer general enquiries about an individual's service. Permanent records of leave taken by RAF personnel are not maintained. Records of officers' emoluments are retained indefinitely, but the pay records of airmen are destroyed after three years. See also Medical Records, p 22; Addresses, p 33.

To whom available

Details will only be given to a solicitor acting on behalf of the individual concerned with his written authority. In other cases they will be produced on subpoena.

How obtained

All enquiries should be addressed as follows:

Officers PM(AR)1b (RAF)

Airmen P(Man)3e(2)a

RAF Personnel Management Centre, Building 248, RAF Innsworth, Glos GL3 1EZ.

Powers of attorney

Information available

All powers of attorney filed in the Central Office of the Supreme Court between 1882 and 1942 have been transferred to the Public Record Office. Since 1 October 1971 it has not been possible to file powers of attorney, and those filed between 1943 and then have been destroyed.

To whom available

Anyone may search and inspect.

How obtained

Application should be made in person to:

Public Record Office, Chancery Lane, London WC2A 1LR (Tel: 081–876 3444).

Cost

Search fee: none. Copies: according to size and method of reproduction.

Admissibility in evidence

Certified copies under the seal of the Public Record Office are admissible in evidence (Public Records Act 1958, s 9).

Enduring powers of attorney

Information available

When an enduring power of attorney has been registered with the Court of Protection (or if there is a pending application to register) full details of the power, including donor, attorney(s) etc, are available.

To whom available

Anyone may search.

How obtained

By postal application on Form EP4 to:

Court of Protection, Stewart House, 24 Kingsway, London WC2B 6JX (Tel: 071–269 7000). Forms will be sent on receipt of a telephoned request.

Requests for copies of a power are considered by the Court and will be granted only if good reason can be shown.

Cost

Search fee £10 to accompany the Form EP4.

Wards of court

Information available

A Ward Book is maintained in which the names of all wards are recorded, so it can be ascertained whether a particular infant is a ward.

To whom available

Anyone with a bona fide interest may enquire.

How obtained

Enquiry should be made in person at:

> Principal Registry, Family Division, Somerset House, London WC2R 1LP.

An official will look at the book and give the information.

Cost

There is no fee.

Wills

Living persons

Information available

The full names of every person who has deposited a will at the Principal Probate Registry during his lifetime since 1858 are available. The register also gives the date of the deposit of the will, and the testator's address at that time. A note appears against the entries relating to wills which have subsequently been admitted to probate. In no circumstances will the contents of a will be divulged unless and until it is proved.

To whom available

Anyone may inspect.

How obtained

A personal search may be made at:

> Principal Registry, Family Division, Room 29, Somerset House, Strand, London WC2R 1LP (Tel: 071–936 6000).

An official search will be made on application by letter addressed to the Record Keeper at the Principal Probate Registry.

Cost

Personal search, free. Official search, 50p.

Proved wills

Information available

The entire contents of a will admitted to probate in England and Wales since 11 January 1858 are available for public inspection and full copies may be obtained.

Information is also available in *A Simplified Guide to Probate Jurisdictions: Where to Look for Wills* by J S W Gibson (Federation of Family History Societies).

To whom available

Anyone may search and inspect.

How obtained

A personal search is made in the annual calendars kept at:

Principal Registry, Family Division, Somerset House, Strand, London WC2R 1LP (Tel: 071–936 6000).

When the reference has been found a copy of the will is produced and may be inspected in the Reading Room. Searchers may take brief notes in pencil. Generally, a will proved in a district probate registry may also be inspected there, as well as at the Principal Registry. There are exceptions and it is advisable to enquire in advance of the district registry in question or of the Record Keeper at the Principal Registry.

Postal applications for searches and copies should be sent to:

The Chief Clerk, Probate Subregister, Duncombe Place, York YO1 2EA.

Cost

Search: in person, free; by post, £2 to include copy will and grant. Inspection of document: 25p. Copies: 25p per page.

Probate and letters of administration

Information available

Calendars at the Principal Registry record every grant, its date, the registry out of which it was issued, and the name and address of the deceased. Calendars prior to 1968 also give the personal representatives' name. Grants issued before 3 August 1981 show the value of the estate. Later ones state that the value is below a certain figure. Copies of the grants may also be inspected and copies obtained.

To whom available

Anyone may inspect.

How obtained

Personal inspection is made at:

Principal Registry, Family Division, Somerset House, Strand, London WC2R 1LP (Tel: 071–936 6000).

Applications for copies may be sent by post to:

The Chief Clerk, Probate Subregister, Duncombe Place, York YO1 2EA.

Cost

Search: in person, free; by post, £2 to include copy will and grant. Inspection of document: 25p. Copies: 25p per page.

Addresses

Civilians

The Department of Social Security has a recorded address for almost every person in the country over the age of 15. The address will only be divulged, however, to clerks of magistrates' courts in maintenance, guardianship of infants and affiliation cases, and to registrars of the Family Division of the High Court in similar cases. The address is then only given on the understanding that it is used for the proceedings and that every reasonable effort has been made to trace the person by other means. In magistrates' courts proceedings the address will not be divulged to the other party or his or her solicitor. In High Court proceedings, the registrar will inform the solicitor, or the litigant if acting in person.

Registrars of the Family Division can also obtain addresses from National Health Service records at the request of wife litigants. An address is recorded for everyone registered to receive general medical services under the National Health Service. The address is only normally revised on a change of doctor, and may therefore be out of date. The following information should if possible be supplied to the registrar: the husband's full name, date of birth, NHS number (if known), present and previous home addresses with dates. No fee is charged.

Soldiers

The addresses of soldiers will not normally be divulged by the Ministry of Defence (Army Department). To facilitate civil litigation, however, addresses will be furnished to solicitors upon their undertaking that the address will only be used by them or their agents for the service of process and will not be divulged to their clients or any other person. A solicitor employed by a public authority or private company should undertake, instead of that the address will not be divulged to his client, that as far as possible it will not be disclosed to any other part of his employer's organisation. In the absence of an undertaking, an indication will be given as to whether the soldier is currently serving in England, Scotland, Northern Ireland or abroad. A letter will be forwarded to the last recorded address of the soldier.

Requests for addresses, or letters for forwarding, should be sent in the case of other ranks to the Record Office of the appropriate Regiment or Corps (addresses in the *Army List*), and in the case of officers to:

Ministry of Defence (AODO), London Rd, Stanmore, Middx HA7 4PZ.

Sailors

Addresses of Royal Naval personnel will only be disclosed for the service of process, as for soldiers (see above), and requests should be addressed as follows:

Royal Navy and WRNS officers   Ministry of Defence (Naval Secretary), Old Admiralty Building, Spring Gardens, London SW1A 2BE.

Royal Navy, WRNS and QARNNS ratings   The Commodore (Naval Drafting Division), HMS Centurion, Grange Rd, Gosport, Hants PO13 9XA.

Royal Navy medical and dental officers   Ministry of Defence, Medical Director General (Naval), First Avenue House, High Holborn, London WC1V 6HE.

QARNNS officers   Ministry of Defence, The Matron-in-Chief QARNNS, First Avenue House, High Holborn, London WC1V 6HE.

Naval chaplains   Ministry of Defence, Chaplain of the Fleet, Lacon House, Theobalds Rd, London WC1T 8RY.

Royal Marine officers   DRMOA, Ripley Block, Old Admiralty Building, Spring Gardens, London SW1A 2BE.

Royal Marine other ranks   The Commodore (DRORM), HMS Centurion, Grange Rd, Gosport, Hants PO13 9XA.

Records of merchant seamen who served in British registered ships of 200 tons and upwards under agreements beginning or ending in the United Kingdom during the period 1941 to 1972 are kept by:

The Registrar General of Shipping and Seamen, Block 2, Government Buildings, St Agnes Road, Gabalfa, Cardiff CF4 4YA (Tel: 0222 586170).

A search may be requested by post; (fee £11). The seaman's name and date and place of birth should be given, and (if known) the number of his discharge book.

Home addresses will not be divulged, but the Registrar General will forward a sealed unstamped letter to the last recorded address of the seaman.

Airmen

Addresses of Royal Air Force personnel will be disclosed only for the purpose of serving process, as for Army personnel (see above). Requests should be addressed as follows:

Officers   PM(AR)1b (RAF)

Airmen   P(Man)3e(2)a

RAF Personnel Management Centre, Building 248, RAF Innsworth, Glos GL3 1EZ.

The Headquarters of the United States Air Force in Britain will attempt to provide the last known address of an American airman stationed or formerly stationed here. If possible, enquiries should give the serviceman's full name, rank, unit and service number. No fee is charged. Requests should be addressed to:

Headquarters, Third Air Force, Office of the Staff Judge Advocate, RAF Mildenhall, Bury St Edmunds, Suffolk IP28 8NF.

Generally

Information available

The addresses of many well-known people are recorded in *Who's Who* (A & C Black Ltd). Those of some company directors are in *The Directory of Directors* (Reed Information Services). Many published lists of members of professions (see p 117) give addresses.

Missing persons

Information available

The Red Cross will assist in tracing missing persons in a limited class of cases. The service is international and only offered in compassionate cases to trace relatives missing as a result of wars, major disasters or similar events. Enquiries will not be made solely for the purpose of legal proceedings. The address of a missing person if found will not be divulged without his consent.

How obtained

Enquiries with full particulars and a stamped addressed envelope for reply should be sent in the first place to:

The Director, International Welfare Department, British Red Cross Society, 9 Grosvenor Crescent, London SW1X 7EJ (Tel: 071–235 5454).

Cost

There is no fee, but a donation is appreciated.

Diplomatic privilege

Information available

The Foreign and Commonwealth Office will state whether any person is notified as a member of a diplomatic mission, consular post or international organisation, and in what capacity.

To whom available

Anyone may enquire.

How obtained

Enquiries should be addressed by letter to:

Foreign and Commonwealth Office, Protocol Department, Old Admiralty Building, Whitehall, London SW1A 2AZ.

Cost

There is no fee.

Pedigrees

Information available

The College of Arms has authenticated pedigrees of many families, including some not aspiring to the degree of distinction that might be supposed necessary for such recording. The Society of Genealogists has a collection of similar records.

To whom available

Anyone may enquire.

How obtained

Enquiries should be addressed by letter to:

College of Arms, Queen Victoria Street, London EC4V 2BT (Tel: 071–248 2762) (who will supply transcriptions of records), or

Society of Genealogists, 14 Charterhouse Buildings, Goswell Road, London EC1M 7BA (Tel: 071–251 8799).

Cost

The charge varies according to the work entailed.

Census returns

Public Record Office

Information available

The returns from the censuses of 1841, 1851, 1861, 1871, 1881 and 1891 are available for inspection at the Public Record Office. Microfilm copies are held by many county record offices. These are the returns made by householders as distinct from the general reports and analyses of the results published by those taking the censuses. The entries are arranged according to the place from which the returns were made and, in the later censuses, the entry relating to each person gives name, age in years, the address of the house where he or she was residing, and relationship to the head of the household, or other reason for residing there (eg servant) and trade or employment. In the older censuses, there was less detail, and it is not always possible to identify the house in which a named person lived. The equivalent Scottish records, for censuses up to 1891, are held by the General Register Office.

To whom available

Anyone may search. At the Public Record Office a reader's ticket is required.

How obtained

Personal or postal application should be made to:

Public Record Office, Chancery Lane, London WC2A 1LR (Tel: 081–876 3444).

The date of the census and the place of residence of the person in whom the enquirer is interested should be given. An application to a county record office should be in person.

In Scotland, an applicant may carry out a general search of census records, or on supplying sufficient identifying information, an extract will be found officially. Application is made to:

General Register Office for Scotland, New Register House, Edinburgh EH1 3YT (Tel: 031–334 0380).

Cost

Public Record Office, no fee; a search fee by officers will be quoted on request. County record offices, generally no fee. General Register Office for Scotland, extract for which identification given, £14; general search by applicant, £15 per day, but copies are then only £6.

General Register Office

Information available

The returns for the censuses taken in 1901, 1911, 1921 and 1951 are arranged in the same way as the previous censuses mentioned under Public Record Office, above and contain the same information. These records are regarded as confidential. The Registrar General is only prepared to consider the release from the 1901 and 1911 returns of the age and place of birth of named persons, and then only with the written consent of the person concerned or a direct descendant.

To whom available

Subject to the restrictions noted above, information may be made available to any enquirer.

How obtained

An application form should be requested from:

CAS Room 115, St Catherines House, 10 Kingsway, London WC2B 6JP (Tel: 071–396 2393 extn 2008).

Cost

The fee is fixed on a time cost basis. Fee for each address in each year, payable at the time of the application: £19.80, incl VAT if enquirer is resident in UK.

Electors

Information available

The register of electors for each district shows against every address the name of the persons living there, or otherwise qualified in respect of that address, entitled to vote at parliamentary, European parliament or local government elections. It is published by 15 February each year. Names of those qualified as electors omitted from the register as first published can be added during the year. By 28 November each year draft registers or electors lists are published from which the following year's register is compiled. Separate parts of this show those newly qualified to be electors, and those who have ceased to be qualified or whose qualification has changed.

To whom available

Anyone may inspect.

How obtained

The register and the list (until the publication of the register compiled from it) may be consulted at the offices of the registration officer (usually the local authority offices). They are usually also available in main post offices in the area covered and in other

public buildings (eg public libraries). Copies can be bought if
there are sufficient available.

Cost

There is no inspection fee. The charges for copies depend on the
number of electors.

Aliens and Commonwealth citizens

Information available

The Home Office Immigration Department has records of aliens,
and Commonwealth citizens subject to control under the Immigration Act 1971, entering the country, and addresses for those
who are obliged to report them. In individual cases information
may be more extensive. Normally this is all regarded as confidential and not disclosed. An address will, however, be divulged, if
known, for serving legal process or executing a warrant, on the
understanding that it will be used for no other purpose. Information may sometimes be given for other purposes, but this is
discretionary.

To whom available

Any solicitor may apply.

How obtained

Application should be made in writing to:

> The Under Secretary of State, Home Office, Lunar House,
> Wellesley Road, Croydon CR9 2BY (Tel: 081–686 0688).

Cost

No charge is made, unless it is agreed that an official is to attend
court to give evidence.

Personal finance

Bankruptcy

Bankruptcy search

Information available

Details of the institution and progress of bankruptcy proceedings against any person are available.

To whom available

The registers noted below are available for inspection by anyone. If a bankruptcy order is recorded, application may be made to the registrar to inspect the file of the proceedings. He has a discretion whether to allow such an inspection; if the applicant appears on the file, ie as debtor or a creditor, access will be allowed.

How obtained

Registers of all petitions and bankruptcy orders, disputed statutory demands and interim orders (and pre-1986 receiving orders, etc) for the whole of the UK are maintained at:

> The Central Bankruptcy Search Room, 9th Floor, Commercial Union House, 22 Martineau Square, Birmingham B2 4UZ (Tel: 021–233 4808/236 8831; fax: 021–233 4960).

These may be searched by telephone, letter or fax (which is preferred). A fax search submitted by, say, 10 am will usually be replied to, by fax, the same day. The name of the debtor, and address and approximate date are ideally required.

Registers of petitions and bankruptcy orders from about 1972, and disputed statutory demands and interim orders for at least the last 18 months are at:

Thomas More Building, Royal Courts of Justice, Strand, London WC2R 1LP. Room 309 (petitions, orders), room 211 (statutory demands and interim orders). (Tel: 071–936 6441.)

These registers relate only to proceedings in London, however. All proceedings outside London will be kept at the county court concerned.

The presentation of a petition and the making of a bankruptcy order will also be revealed (within five years of registration unless renewed) by making a search at the Land Charges Registry (see next section).

Cost

Personal search at Thomas More Building: £1 per hour. Searches at the Central Search Room, no charge.

Land Charges Registry

Information available

The presentation of bankruptcy petitions and making of receiving orders are recorded in the Land Charges Department of HM Land Registry. The record is alphabetical under the bankrupt's name.

To whom available

Anyone may search.

How obtained

A postal search may be made by sending Form K16 to:

The Superintendent, Land Charges Department, Burrington Way, Plymouth PL5 3LP.

The telephone and fax search facilities are available to persons with a key number: Tel: 0752 701171; fax: 0752 766666.

Cost

Search fee, £1 per name.

Bills of sale

Information available

Bills of sale must be registered at the Central Office of the Supreme Court (Room E07) and a search may be made and particulars taken. Copies are also supplied. As well as the bills, the affidavits of execution and renewal may be inspected and copies obtained.

To whom available

Anyone may search.

How obtained

Personal attendance is necessary although a requisition for an official search can be made. An alphabetical index is maintained under the surnames of the grantors, and a note is added when a notice of satisfaction is filed. Where the grantor has an address outside the London bankruptcy area an additional copy is forwarded to the registrar of the county court for the district concerned, and a search may be carried out in the county court as well.

Cost

Personal search: 5p for each name; official search: £2 for one name, £1 for each subsequent name; continuation search within one month: £1.

Deeds of arrangement

Information available

Deeds of arrangement that have been registered (both pre- and post-Insolvency Act) are available. In addition, accounts of receipts and payments, dividend lists and trading accounts (or, if applicable, affidavits of no receipts and payments) are filed annually and when the trustee closes an estate.

To whom available

Anyone may search for the information regarding the deed. The accounts and other documents are available only from the trustee or supervisor, and at his discretion.

How obtained

To obtain details of the name and address of the debtor, the date of the deed and the name and address of the supervisor or trustee, application may be made by telephone to:

Insolvency Service, Commercial Union House, 22 Martineau Square, Birmingham B2 4UZ (Tel: 021–233 4808).

Anyone wishing to inspect the deed itself will need to attend in person at the county court concerned (in London, the High Court), where a copy is available.

Cost

Insolvency Service, no charge. High or county court, no charge for inspection. Trustees or supervisors may charge for documents they supply.

Agricultural credits

Information available

Upon the creation of a fixed or floating charge on a farmer's agricultural assets, which various Acts authorise notwithstanding the statutory provisions relating to bills of sale, brief particulars are registered at a special department of HM Land Registry. They are indexed alphabetically under the farmers' names and give the names of the chargees. A postal official search reveals a reference to any registration and particulars are obtained from an office copy of the entry.

To whom available

Anyone may search.

How obtained

A personal search and inspection can be made at:

Land Charges Department, Burrington Way, Plymouth PL5 3LP.

An official search may be made on the prescribed form (AC6) giving the name and address of the farmer. Office copies may also be applied for by post (on Form AC5). Postal applications should be addressed to the Agricultural Credits Superintendent.

Cost

Search 50p. Office copy, £1. Fees include value added tax, and tax invoices are supplied on request.

Proprietors of registered land

Information available

The Index of Proprietors' Names kept by HM Land Registry records the title numbers of any registered land, or charges and incumbrances secured on registered land, of which any person alone is registered as proprietor, arranged alphabetically under surnames. Before November 1977 limited companies and other corporations were not included, nor were persons holding jointly with others. Some, but by no means all, of those excluded proprietors who have owned the land since before November 1977 have now been entered on the index.

To whom available

Only the proprietor himself and other persons satisfying the Chief Land Registrar of their proper interest in the property may search. Such other persons have to have an 'ownership interest', eg a trustee in bankruptcy or a personal representative, whose interest is in the whole of the property of the proprietor concerned.

How obtained

Application for an official search should be made by letter to:

The Chief Land Registrar, HM Land Registry, Burrington Way, Plymouth PL5 3LP (Tel: 0752 779831).

The letter should give the full names against which a search is required, and particulars of the applicant's interest.

Cost

Search fee, £16 per name payable in advance.

County court judgments

Information available

Every county court judgment for £1 and over (usually to a maximum of £5,000) which has not within one month (from judgment or taxation if later) been satisfied wholly, or in part so as to leave less than £1 outstanding, is registered centrally. Administration orders made in county courts are also registered. Where a registered judgment is reversed or set aside by the county court or on appeal, the entry in the register is cancelled. Where a registered judgment is complied with, any party to the action can obtain a cancellation of the entry by application to the court in which the judgment was obtained. As this involves a separate application it may be overlooked, so that the fact that a judgment is registered does not automatically mean that it is unsatisfied. The records are kept for six years. Certified copy entries may be obtained. The registration gives the name and address of the person against whom judgment was given, the amount and date of judgment, the name of the court and the plaint number of the action. There is no reference to the plaintiff in the action.

To whom available

Anyone may search the register.

How obtained

A personal search may be made at:

Registry of County Court Judgments, Registry Trust Ltd, 173–175 Cleveland Street, London W1P 5PE (Tel: 071–830 0133).

The register is now arranged alphabetically in yearly sections.

An official search will be made on application by letter addressed to the Registry.

Cost

Personal search £4 per name; postal £4.50. Certified copy entry, £4.

War-time debtors

Information available

The Deeds of Arrangement Registry keeps a register of debtors who made schemes of arrangement, or on whom protection orders and adjustment orders were made by county courts under the Liabilities (War-time Adjustment) Acts 1941 and 1944. The name, address and occupation of the debtor are given, along with the dates of making and revoking schemes and orders, and the name of the county court concerned.

To whom available

Anyone may search.

How obtained

A search against a particular name may be made by post or telephone to:

Insolvency Service, Commercial Union House, 22 Martineau Square, Birmingham B2 4UZ (Tel: 021–233 4808).

Cost

No fee.

Bank and building society accounts

Information available

Banks and building societies are obliged to maintain strict confidentiality about their customers' affairs. Many are, however, prepared to assist the personal representatives of a deceased person to trace accounts held by the deceased, provided that the secrecy rules are not broken. This means that, in the first instance, the information provided (if it is provided) will be limited to confirmation that an account in the name of the deceased has been traced. All will consider any request. Building societies are largely computerised in terms of lists of account holders, and are thus able to ascertain the information relatively easily; not all banks are.

To whom available

Personal representatives and (preferably) their solicitors.

How obtained

Application must be made in writing. The full name of the deceased and an address or addresses should be given and a copy of the death certificate provided. Any other useful information should be added. In the first instance application should be made to the local branch, which will refer the request to head office if need be.

Cost

Normally no charge, but this can depend on the ease with which the bank or building society can ascertain the information requested. Some will make a charge.

Credit cards

These are fully computerised and a request to the main issuing office should lead to the requested information being provided.

Real property

Registration of title

Information available

One may discover from HM Land Registry whether the title to any piece of land in England and Wales is registered. If so, all the entries on the register may be inspected, and also the filed plan and filed documents referred to on the register. Accordingly, there are revealed the extent of the land, the type of title, details of the rights registered as appurtenant to it or subject to which it is held, charges and other incumbrances affecting it, the names, addresses and descriptions of the registered proprietor of the land and charges on it, and registered notices, cautions and restrictions. This information can be obtained by personal search or from office copies. A personal searcher will also be told whether there are any pending applications affecting the title. If a postal search is made, on the official form, details will be given of any adverse entries made on the register after a date inserted on the form by the searcher, and of any pending application.

To whom available

Since 3 December 1990 the registers have been open to inspection by any member of the public.

How obtained

Both personal and postal searches should be made at the appropriate district land registry according to the location of the land, as follows:

Birkenhead   (Cheshire, London Boroughs of Hammersmith

& Fulham and Kensington & Chelsea, Merseyside, Staffs) Old Market House, Hamilton Street, Birkenhead, Merseyside L41 5FL (Tel: 051–473 1110 (1106 enquiries)).

Coventry (West Midlands) Greyfriars Business Centre, 2 Eaton Road, Coventry CV1 2SD (Tel: 0203 632442).

Croydon (London Boroughs of Bexley, Bromley, Croydon and Sutton) Sunley House, Bedford Park, Croydon CR9 3LE (Tel: 081–781 9100 (9103 enquiries)).

Durham (Cleveland, Cumbria, Durham, Northumberland, Surrey, Tyne and Wear) Southfield House, Southfield Way, Durham DH1 5TR (Tel: 091–301 3500).

Gloucester (Berks, Glos, Oxon, Warwicks, Wilts) Bruton Way, Gloucester GL1 1DQ (Tel: 0452 511111).

Harrow (London Boroughs of Barnet, Brent, Camden, Harrow, Islington, Cities of London and Westminster, Inner & Middle Temples) Lyon House, Lyon Road, Harrow, Middx HA1 2EU (Tel: 081–427 8811).

Kingston-upon-Hull (Humberside, Lincs, Norfolk, Suffolk) Earle House, Hull HU2 8JN (Tel: 0482 223244).

Leicester (Bucks, Leics) Thames Tower, 99 Burleys Way, Leicester LE1 3UB (Tel: 0533 654000).

Lytham (Greater Manchester, Lancs) Birkenhead House, East Beach, Lytham St Annes, Lancashire FY8 5AB (Tel: 0253 736999 (739661 enquiries)).

Nottingham (Derbyshire, Notts, South Yorks, West Yorks) Chalfont Drive, Nottingham NG8 3RN (Tel: 0602 291166).

Peterborough (Beds, Cambs, Essex, Northants) Touthill Close, City Road, Peterborough PE1 1XN (Tel: 0733 288288).

Plymouth (Avon, Cornwall, Devon, Scilly Isles, Somerset) Plumer House, Tailyour Road, Crownhill, Plymouth PL6 5HY (Tel: 0752 701234).

Portsmouth (East Sussex, Isle of Wight) St Andrewts Court, St Michael's Road, Portsmouth, Hampshire PO1 2JH (Tel: 0705 865022).

Stevenage (London Boroughs of Barking & Dagenham,

Enfield, Hackney, Haringey, Havering, Newham, Redbridge, Tower Hamlets and Waltham Forest, Herts) Brickdale House, Swingate, Stevenage, Hertfordshire SG1 1XG (Tel: 0438 313003 (315464 enquiries)).

Swansea (Clwyd, Dyfed, London Boroughs of Ealing, Hillingdon and Hounslow, Gwent, Gwynedd, Hereford and Worcester, Mid Glamorgan, Powys, South Glamorgan, West Glamorgan) Ty Cym Tawe, Phoenix Way, Llansamlet, Swansea SA7 9FQ (for titles in Wales), Ty Bryn Glas, High Street, Swansea SA1 1PW (for other titles) (Tel: 0792 458877, for both offices).

Telford (London Boroughs of Greenwich, Kingston upon Thames, Lambeth, Lewisham, Merton, Richmond upon Thames, Southwark and Wandsworth, Shropshire) Parkside Court, Hall Park Way, Telford TF3 4LR (Tel: 0952 290355).

Tunbridge Wells (Kent) Curtis House, Hawkenbury, Tunbridge Wells, Kent TN2 5AQ (Tel: 0892 510015).

Weymouth (Dorset, Hants, West Sussex) 1 Cumberland Drive, Weymouth, Dorset DT4 9TT (Tel: 0305 776161).

York (North Yorks) James House, James Street, York YO1 3YZ (Tel: 0904 450000).

The most convenient way to obtain information is to apply by post on Land Registry Form 109, for a copy of the register entries and/or plan, as required. A separate form is needed for each title. If the title number is not known, either a search of the index map may be made on Form 96 or use Form 109 but insert in the space provided for the title number 'Please supply the title number'. Copies of documents referred to on the register may then be obtained by applying on Form 110. In each case the fee(s) must be paid with the application.

Alternatively, anyone may inspect the register in person. Four days' notice should be given, and Form 111 completed at the registry and the fee paid. Again, if the title number is not known, either of the steps outlined above may be taken.

Cost

Search of index map (Form 96) £8; copy of the register or of the title plan (Form 109), £8 each, plus £8 if the title number is unknown; copies of documents (Form 110), £8 per copy or set; personal inspection of the register or the title plan or of any or all documents referred to (Form 111), £8 per title (but no charge to the registered proprietor of the title in question) plus £8 if the title number is not known. Fees should be paid by cheque or postal order or, if in person, in cash. Credit cards cannot be accepted.

Admissibility in evidence

Office copies of and extracts from the register and filed documents and plans are admissible in evidence to the same extent as the originals (Land Registration Act 1925, s 113).

Land charges

Information available

The five registers kept by the Land Registry concern: pending actions; annuities (no registrations after 1925); writs and orders affecting land; deeds of arrangement affecting land (which are also registered with other deeds of arrangement: see p 41); and land charges. Entries give brief particulars of the matters capable of registration, usually including: type of registration, land affected (plans can be, but seldom are, registered), name of the estate owner whose interest is affected, parties to the deeds or action concerned, and the person making the registration, with solicitors, if any. Entries do not affect land to which the title is registered.

To whom available

Anyone may search.

How obtained

An alphabetical index of estate owners is maintained on computer, referring to entries on all the registers. A personal search may be made at:

Land Charges Department, Burrington Way, Plymouth PL5 3LP (Searches, by solicitors and others with credit facilities:

Tel: 0752 701177. Fax: 766666. Administration: Tel: 0752 779831).

At Plymouth, entries revealed on the index may be inspected.

An official search is applied for by post to Plymouth on Form K15, addressed to the Superintendent, and office copies are obtained of any entry revealed on sending Form K19.

Cost

Official search, £1 per name. Office copy £1. Telephone, telex or fax search £2 per name.

Admissibility in evidence

An office copy is admissible in all proceedings to the same extent as the original (Land Charges Act 1972, s 1(5)).

Local land charges

Information available

The register of local land charges is divided into twelve parts, as follows:

Part I General financial charges. These normally concern works done by a local authority which will have power to charge a specific sum on the land, in cases where the sum is not yet ascertained.

Part II Specific financial charges. Here the property is charged with a specific sum (sometimes with interest) in favour of the local authority.

Part III Planning restrictions or prohibitions as to use. This concerns matters registrable under the planning legislation before 1947, and restrictions applying to particular pieces of land under the later planning legislation, such as enforcement notices, and building and tree preservation orders.

Part IV Other restrictions or prohibitions as to use. Examples of matters registrable here are improvement and building lines, voluntary agreements with local authorities restricting user and orders relating to ancient monuments.

Part V   Charges for the upkeep of private ways in fenland.

Part VI   Compulsory purchase orders under the Town and Country Planning Act 1944, and those containing a direction for expedited procedure.

Part VII   Compulsory purchase and designation orders for new towns.

Part VIII   Orders and directions imposing restrictions for the safety of aircraft and efficient working of aerodromes.

Part IX   Compulsory purchase and rights orders in connection with opencast mining.

Part X   Lists of buildings of special architectural or historic interest.

Part XI   Light obstruction notices under the Rights of Light Act 1959.

Part XII   Particulars of areas affected by schemes under the Land Drainage Act 1961.

The matters registrable in the local land charges registers are numerous and varied. The particulars normally revealed on a search are: the nature of the charge, date imposed, by what order or instrument, where that may be inspected, sum of money secured if appropriate, in whose favour the charge is registered, and the date of registration. Further information and copies of documents referred to will usually be given on request.

To whom available

Anyone may search.

How obtained

The register is kept by the district council or London borough council in whose area the land lies. Applications for searches may be made either in person at the council offices, or by post on the form of requisition for an official search (LLC1). The form must be completed to identify the land (if necessary a plan should be sent) and specify the parts of the register to be searched (if not all). The addresses of the authorities to which searches should be submitted are given in the *Longman Directory of Local Authorities* (Longman, 1993).

Cost

Although there are recommended fees, most authorities fix their
own levels and enquiry should be made of them.

Planning

Information available

The address of any property in respect of which a planning application has been made (at any time since 1947), the details of the
applicant and the application, and the result. There is also a
register of enforcement and stop notices served by the planning
authority, giving details of the property address and the person
against whom enforcement etc is sought.

To whom available

Anyone may search.

How obtained

By personal visit to the local planning authority. Alternatively,
the details regarding a specific property could be requested by
post.

Cost

Search, free. For copies, a straight copying charge may be made.
There is an additional enquiry concerning these registers that
forms part of the local authority search, and in that case the
appropriate fee will be charged.

Listed buildings

Information available

Complete lists of all 'listed' buildings, ie buildings of special architectural or historic interest situated in England.

To whom available

Anyone may search.

How obtained

The complete lists are held by:

National Buildings Record Office, Fortress House, 23 Savile Row, London W1X 2JQ (Tel: 071–973 3091). Monday–Friday 10 am to 5.30 pm. Personal visits are recommended.

Alternatively, London borough councils, district councils and county and district planning authorities all hold the list(s) covering buildings in their area. These can be inspected by anyone. The National Office provides listings by county/district/parish and there are various guides and gazetteers to assist in locating the object of the search, and a queries desk for basic information.

Cost

Search, free. Copies from the National Office are 20p a sheet ('do it yourself'); local authorities' charges vary.

Land ownership

Unused or underused public land

Information available

A register of land belonging to certain public bodies which the Secretary of State regards as unused or insufficiently used is kept by him. He sends each local authority a copy of the register relating to its area. The bodies owning the land include the Crown, local authorities, statutory undertakers, and specified nationalised industries.

To whom available

Anyone may search.

How obtained

Application should be made in person to the principal office of
the local authority for the area.

Cost

Inspection, free. Copies, at a reasonable charge determined by
the council.

Land value duty records

Information available

For the purpose of land value duty, introduced by the Finance
(1909–10) Act 1910, but abandoned shortly afterwards, a comprehensive survey of all land was prepared by the Inland Revenue
showing the owner, occupier, acreage and rateable value of each
separate plot. The plots can be identified by reference to an
accompanying Ordnance Survey map. The information generally
relates to ownership on one occasion shortly before the First
World War.

To whom available

Anyone may search.

How obtained

Application should be made to the county record office for the
area in question.

Cost

Generally, no charge is made for access to the records.

Yorkshire Deeds Registries

Information available

Particulars or copies of deeds and other documents disposing of
a legal estate in land within the three former Ridings of Yorkshire
(but not the City of York) had to be registered in the appropriate

Riding deeds registry. The West and North Riding registries were closed to registrations in 1970 and the East Riding registry in 1976. Leases for terms not exceeding twenty-one years, where the lessee took possession, and dealings with those short leases, and all deeds relating to land with a registered title, were excluded. The memorials and copies may be inspected and copies obtained.

To whom available

Anyone may search.

How obtained

Searches may be made personally, or requested by post. The records offices will accept requests by telephone if sufficiently precise—

East Riding Humberside County Record Office, County Hall, Beverley, North Humberside HU17 9BA (Tel: 0482 867131). Personal searchers are requested to give prior notice.

North Riding County Archivist, North Yorkshire County Record Office, County Hall, Northallerton, North Yorks DL7 8AD (Tel: 0609 777585). All visitors must make appointments.

West Riding West Yorkshire Archives Service Headquarters, Registry of Deeds, Newstead Road, Wakefield WF1 2DE (Tel: 0924 295982).

Cost

East Riding Searches, free. Copies: 50p per sheet plus VAT up to £2, thereafter £2.35 (office copy) or £3.53 (certified copy) per document incl VAT.

North Riding Search by staff £13 an hour, min £6.50. Copies: £10.90 handling charge per volume of deeds handled plus 18p per frame of microfiche, 20p per A4 print-out, plus postage and VAT.

West Riding Copies of documents: if registration particulars are supplied, £10 for an office copy, £15 a certified copy; without those particulars, £22 per office copy, £27 per certified copy.

Middlesex Deeds Registry

Information available

Information from the memorials of deeds registered in the Middlesex Deeds Registry is still available, despite the closing of the registry. Memorials show the date and nature of the deed and the parties to it, and identify the land affected. There are not generally any details of restrictive covenants.

To whom available

Anyone may inspect.

How obtained

Registers of memorials and related indexes, from 1709 to 1935, may be inspected without prior notice at:

Greater London Record Office, 40 Northampton Road, London EC1R 0HB (Tel: 071–332 3820) Tuesday–Friday, 9.30 am to 4.45 pm (7.30 Tuesdays).

Black and white photographs of records can be ordered, but photocopies are not available.

Cost

There is no search fee.

Bedford Level Deeds Registry

Information available

Conveyances and leases for over seven years, or not in possession, of any part of an area of 95,000 acres of the fens drained in the seventeenth century, known as 'adventurers' lands' in the Bedford Level, had to be registered with the Bedford Level Corporation. Wills affecting the title to that land also had to be registered.

Registrations started in 1649 (for conveyances) and 1664 (for leases), and formally ended in 1920 when the Corporation was abolished, though from about 1860 the registration requirement was often disregarded.

To whom available

Anyone may search.

How obtained

Searches may be made personally at:

County Record Office, Shire Hall, Cambridge CB3 0AP (Tel: 0223 317281).

Notice of an intended visit is helpful, but not essential. Limited postal searches are carried out by staff.

Cost

There is no charge for the use of the records. Copies: 20p (A4 size), 30p (A3 size), plus handling charges where appropriate.

Enrolled deeds

Information available

The contents of enrolled deeds may be inspected and copies obtained. Few deeds are now enrolled because of the repeal of the provisions making it necessary, but it may prove useful to inspect deeds formerly enrolled.

To whom available

Anyone may search and inspect.

How obtained

Personal application should be made to the appropriate office according to the enactment under which the deed was enrolled:

Central Office of the Supreme Court, Royal Courts of Justice, Room E07, Strand, London WC2A 2LL (Tel: 071–936

6000). Records of deeds enrolled here are transferred to the Public Record Office three years after enrolment.

The Charity Commissioners, St Albans House, 57–60 Haymarket, London SW1Y 4QX (Tel: 071–210 4477).

The Office of Land Revenue Records and Enrolments. This is now superseded by the Public Record Office, Chancery Lane, London WC2A 1LR (Tel: 081–876 3444).

The Office of the Duchy of Cornwall, 10 Buckingham Gate, London SW1E 6LA (Tel: 071–834 7346).

The Office of the Duchy of Lancaster, Lancaster Place, London WC2E 7ED (Tel: 071–836 8277).

Cost

Fees vary according to the office and the length of the deed.

Manorial records

Information available

The last known location of certain types of manorial documents (records of manorial courts but not muniments of title) is recorded on the Manorial Register, kept by the Historical Manuscripts Commission. Where there is no trace on the register, assistance may be derived from the appropriate county record office. The documents themselves may be in private hands, when access will depend upon the owner's permission.

To whom available

Anyone may consult the register.

How obtained

It is advisable to inspect the Manorial Register personally at the offices of:

Historical Manuscripts Commission, Quality House, Quality Court, Chancery Lane, London WC2A 1HP (Tel: 071–242 1198).

The search room is open Monday–Friday, 9.30 am to 5.00 pm. Limited information will be given by post, but the staff can undertake no research.

The register is arranged by counties, so the county in which the manor lies must be known. There is an alphabetical list of parishes with the names of the manors that lie within them.

Cost

There is no fee.

Commons

Information available

All common land (ie land subject to rights of common, or manorial waste land) and all town or village greens (land allotted or used for recreation by local inhabitants) are registered. The New Forest, Epping Forest and the Forest of Dean are not included. The registers show the persons claiming or found to be the owners of such land, and the rights of common exercisable over it.

To whom available

Anyone may search.

How obtained

Application is made in person or by post to the registration authority, which is the county council of the area where the land is situated. A requisition must be made on the prescribed form, obtainable from the registration authority.

Cost

Search fee, £6. Copies, £6 for the register entry and plan.

Ordnance survey maps

Old editions

Information available

All out of print editions of Ordnance Survey maps may be inspected in and copies obtained from the Map Library of the British Library.

To whom available

Anyone over the age of 21 may inspect and obtain copies.

How obtained

The plans and maps may be inspected in the Map Library of the British Library Reference Division, on the mezzanine floor of the King Edward Building on the north side of the British Museum. A temporary reader's pass must be obtained at the Map Library. The Map Library is open from 10 am to 4.30 pm, Monday–Saturday. Twenty-four hours' notice should be given for inspecting large-scale plans. This may be given by telephone (071–636 1544). Applications for copies may be sent by post to:

The Map Librarian, Map Library, The British Library, Great Russell Street, London WC1B 3DG.

Cost

There is no inspection fee. Copies are charged according to size. Crown copyright subsists in Ordnance Survey maps and plans for fifty years from the end of the year of production. Where copyright applies the Library will notify the applicant, who will have to pay a royalty to the Director General of the Ordnance Survey before the copies are made. (The general licence to reproduce Ordnance maps which solicitors can hold does not cover the royalty on copies made by the Library.) A £13.50 deposit is taken against the royalty and the copies may take a month to prepare. Express services are available, at a premium.

Forthcoming editions

Information available

The Ordnance Survey make available revised survey information
not yet published, for areas covered by published sheets on the
1:1250 and 1:2500 scales. The information can be on paper, microfilm copycards, stable film or 'superplan', direct from a computer
database. Some advance information is held by Ordnance Survey
agents; where this is not sufficiently up to date, a newly com-
missioned copy of the latest information can usually be supplied.
Details may be obtained from:

> The Ordnance Survey, Romsey Road, Maybush, South-
> ampton SO9 4DH (Tel: 0703 792912).

How obtained

Copies may be obtained, in descending order of expense, from
Ordnance Survey head office, their local offices and their commercial agents.

Tithe redemption annuity

Information available

The Tithe Redemption Office records show whether tithe redemption annuity was payable in respect of any piece of land, and if
so its amount and reference number. Brief details of corn rents
and corn rent annuities are also given where these are known to
have been payable, but the records do not always show whether
particular parcels are charged. The persons entitled to receive the
corn rents are named, and enquiry should be made of them.
All tithe maps and apportionments and other records have been
transferred to the Public Record Office.

To whom available

Anyone may search, but at the Public Record Office a reader's
ticket is required.

How obtained

Film copies of the records may be inspected personally at:

Public Record Office, Ruskin Avenue, Kew, Richmond, Surrey TW9 4DN (Tel: 081–876 3444).

Three days' notice may be required to make records available.

The former Inland Revenue records are held at:

Public Record Office, Bourne Avenue, Hayes, Middx UB1 1RF (Tel: 081–573 3831).

They may be inspected there.

Cost

No inspection fee. Copies will be charged according to size and method of reproduction.

Rights of way

Information available

The position of public rights of way is now shown on the maps prepared under the National Parks and Access to the Countryside Act 1949. They are also shown on 1:50,000 Ordnance Survey maps.

To whom available

Anyone may inspect the maps.

How obtained

The statutory maps are kept by the local authority of the area concerned. They may be inspected in person at the offices of the council, or enquiry may be made by letter accompanied by a plan. One of the optional additional questions on the agreed form of enquiries to accompany requisitions for official local land charges searches asks whether the property concerned is crossed by a public right of way. A plan must accompany the requisition if this question is asked.

Cost

Varies between authorities.

Highways

Information available

A list of highways maintainable at the public expense within its area is kept by every district and London borough council.

See also, Quarter Sessions, p 127.

To whom available

Anyone may inspect.

How obtained

The list is available for personal inspection at the offices of the council concerned. Enquiries will also usually be answered through the post. The information from the list is given in answer to one of the agreed standard enquiries to accompany requisitions for official local land charges searches.

Cost

There is no fee.

Street works

Information available

The name and address of any person or body (usually a public utility) proposing to 'open up' a highway, details of the works to be carried out and approximate time; where the works are completed, that information and also details of any faults subsequently occurring and the action taken to reinstate them. The register also includes details of works being done to the highway itself, including those by the highways authority.

It is intended that there will in due course be a national database, to be called the Computerised Roads and Street Works Register (CRSWR), but this is unlikely to be in place before 1995.

To whom available

Anyone may search. Some information on the register is, however, classified as 'restricted' (typically, commercially sensitive information relating, for example, to details of works being done by cable TV companies). This will be restricted to persons having authority to execute works in the street in question or otherwise appearing to the authority to have a sufficient interest.

How obtained

By personal inspection at the authority's offices; it is suggested that an appointment be made.

Cost

No charge is made.

Sewers

Information available

A map showing the positions of public sewers, and sewers which will be adopted as public sewers under declarations by or agreements with the local authority, is available for inspection. Sewers reserved for foul water only or surface water only are specifically marked. Public sewers not so reserved which were vested in the local authority before 1 October 1937, are not necessarily shown.

From April 1992 local authorities could elect whether to retain responsibility for public sewers or to pass it to the water authority. If passed over, the local authority will be responsible only for new sewers until adopted. The register will, however, continue to be maintained by the local authority, albeit based on information fed back to it.

To whom available

Anyone may inspect the map.

How obtained

The maps are open for inspection at the offices of the borough or district council for the area concerned.

Cost

There is no fee.

Trade effluent

Information available

Sewerage undertakers are required to keep and make available copies of all consents given and agreements entered into relating to the discharge of trade effluent, and of all directions given and notices served in relation to them.

To whom available

Anyone may search.

How obtained

The register and documents may be inspected in person at the offices of the appropriate undertaker.

Cost

Inspection, free of charge. A reasonable sum may be charged for copies supplied.

Land drainage

Information available

The Ordnance Survey reference, name of occupier and area (in acres and/or hectares) of all agricultural land and buildings that form a drainage hereditament. Also details of 'maintained watercourses' within each drainage board's area are available.

To whom available

Anyone may search.

How obtained

Apply in writing to the local internal drainage board.

Cost

A fee will be charged depending on the work involved.

Pipelines

Information available

Plans of pipelines authorised to be constructed or diverted under the Pipelines Act 1962 and the Gas Act 1972, showing their route and extent, are open for inspection.

To whom available

Anyone may inspect.

How obtained

Inspection may be made personally at the offices of the local authority for the area concerned. One of the optional additional questions on the agreed form of enquiries to accompany requisitions for official local land charges searches asks whether the property is affected by such a pipeline.

Cost

There is no fee for personal inspection. For enquiry accompanying local land charges search, check with local authority.

Tree preservation orders

Information available

The terms of such orders may be inspected and copies obtained.

They will specify the land affected, the trees concerned, the permission necessary before felling, and the replanting that may be required.

To whom available

Anyone may inspect.

How obtained

The existence of a tree preservation order affecting a particular piece of land will be revealed by a search in Part III of the local land charges register (see p 51). The council concerned will supply a copy of the order on request.

Cost

Copy order, free. Searches in Part III only of the local land charges register, check with local authority.

Trees in conservation areas

Information available

Details of notices served under s 211 of the Town and Country Planning Act 1990 of intention to do anything in respect of a tree in a conservation area *not* covered by a preservation order but which act would be prohibited by such an order.

To whom available

Anyone may enquire.

How obtained

Apply in person or by letter to the local planning authority.

Cost

Free of charge.

Water resources

Information available

Water undertakers must keep records of the location of resource mains, water mains and discharge pipes, and any other underground works other than service pipes, vested in them. The supply companies (if different) maintain a 'quality register', giving details of the constituents of the water being supplied within their area.

To whom available

Anyone may search

How obtained

By personal inspection at the undertaker's (supplier's) offices.

Cost

Inspection, free. A charge may be made for copies.

National Rivers Authority

Information available

The NRA maintains various registers. First, there is that detailing all water abstraction and impounding licences granted. Another consists of the pollution control registers, and contains information about notices of water quality objectives, about samples taken of water or effluent and analyses of them, and consents to discharge effluent. The NRA also keeps maps of the fresh-water limits of rivers and watercourses, a main river map, and records (in map form) of all resource mains and discharge pipes and any other underground works that are for the time being vested in it.

To whom available

Anyone may search.

How obtained

The records may be inspected personally at the regional office of
the NRA.

Cost

No charge for inspection. A charge may be made for copies.

Environmental protection

Information available

Under the Environmental Protection Act 1990 various authorities
are obliged to maintain various registers. Waste regulation
authorities (broadly, metropolitan and county councils, etc) — and
waste collection authorities, if they are not regulation authorities — must record details of all licences granted or being currently
applied for; modifications thereto; any notices issued in relation
to them; convictions of any licence holders, etc.

Principal litter authorities (other than county councils, regional
councils or joint boards) must maintain records of all orders made
by them and of all street litter control notices.

The appropriate licensing authority must keep registers giving full
details of applications for and grants of licences for deposits at
sea and incineration at sea, and also variations and revocations of
such licences.

To whom available

Anyone may inspect.

How obtained

The registers may be inspected in person at the offices of the
relevant authority.

Cost

Inspection, free. A reasonable sum may be charged for copies.

Fencing railway lines

Information available

British Rail Property Board will state whether the railways are under an obligation to fence any particular stretch of track as part of the accommodation works made necessary on the original purchase of the land, or whether their predecessors in title contracted out of the obligation.

To whom available

Any solicitor may apply.

How obtained

Application should be made by letter accompanied by a plan showing the Ordnance Survey plot numbers of the adjacent land to the Property Services Division, British Rail Property Board, for the region concerned as follows:

London and South East Fitzroy House, 355 Euston Road, London NW1 3AG.

Midland Region Stanier House, 10 Holliday Street, Birmingham BT1 1TG.

North Eastern Region Hudson House, Toft Green, York YO1 1HP.

North Western Region 34 High Street, Manchester M1 4OB.

South Western Region Temple Gate House, Temple Gate, Bristol BS1 6PX.

Scotland Scotrail House, 58 Port Dundas Road, Glasgow G4 0HG.

Cost

The Board reserve the right to charge a production fee for consulting the appropriate deeds. This may be waived, so no remittance should be sent with the enquiry.

Chancel repair liability

Information available

Some land is burdened with the obligation to repair the chancel of the local Church of England or Church in Wales parish church, because at some time in the past it belonged to the lay rector of the parish. There are no comprehensive records of which land is affected, but the best seem to be the maps with the tithe records now held by the Public Record Office. Other possible sources of information are the diocesan record office and the parochial church council.

To whom available

Anyone may search, but at the Public Record Office a reader's ticket is required.

How obtained

The records are kept, and may be inspected at:

Public Record Office, Bourne Avenue, Hayes, Middx UB1 1RF and

Public Record Office, Ruskin Avenue, Kew, Richmond, Surrey TW9 4DU (Tel: 081–876 3444).

Three days' notice may be required.

Cost

Search, free.

Coal mining subsidence

Information avaiable

There is statutory right to inspect the National Coal Board's plans showing the workings of coal. The Board's Areas are prepared to give a written mining report covering details of all past, present and future coal mining operations.

To whom available

Anyone may inspect the plans and make enquiries.

How obtained

In the first instance application should be made to:

Technical Department, British Coal, Ashby Road, Stanhope Bretby, Burton-on-Trent, Staffs DE15 0QD (Tel: 0283 550606).

Cost

Mining report submitted on proper form £23.50, otherwise £40.

Brine subsidence

Information available

Whether land is or has been affected by brine subsidence. Applicants will be advised whether the land is in a consultation area (ie an area where the local planning authority, if in receipt of a planning application, will consult the Board to assess the effect of any subsidence, etc), whether a notice of damage has been filed (ie a claim for compensation) and whether that claim has been commuted. The search area covers most but not all of Cheshire.

To whom available

The owner of the land or anyone with his authority.

How obtained

Application should be made in writing giving the full address of the property and accompanied by a location plan, to:

Cheshire Brine Subsidence Compensation Board, 41 Chester Way, Northwich, Cheshire CW9 5JE (Tel: 0606 42172).

Cost

£7.05 incl VAT, to be paid with the application.

Clay mining

Information available

Whether land is affected or may be affected by clay mining activities.

To whom available

Anyone may search.

How obtained

Apply in writing or by fax, accompanied by a plan of the property in question and the surrounding area, to:

English China Clays plc, ECC International, John Keay House, St Austell, Cornwall PL25 4DJ (Tel: 0726 74482; fax: 0726 623019).

Cost

By letter, £28.20 incl VAT; fax, £35.25 incl VAT.

Tin mining

Information available

Whether land is affected or may be affected by tin mining activities in Cornwall.

To whom available

Anyone may apply.

How obtained

Application should be made in writing or by fax, accompanied by a plan identifying the land, to:

Cornish Chamber of Mines, Cornwall Consultants, Gilberts

Coombe, New Portreath Road, Redruth, Cornwall TR15 4HG (Tel: 0209 313511; fax: 0209 313512).

The result of the search will indicate any relevant mining activity and, if felt necessary (in the case of a proposed development, for example) recommend a site investigation.

Cost

For a basic domestic search: £30 plus VAT if clear, £54 plus VAT where there are features that affect (and including an opinion as to the likely effect). For a non-domestic search, £80 plus VAT.

Planning and advertisement regulation applications

Information available

Details of applications for planning permission and consent to the display of advertisements, and whether they were refused or granted with or without conditions, are recorded in registers by the local planning authority for the area concerned. Conditional planning permissions given by the local planning authority (but not by the Secretary of State) may also be registered in Part III of the local land charges register, but the practice is not consistent. Councils will supply copies of their decisions.

To whom available

Anyone may search.

How obtained

As to the local land charges register, see p 51. Application for information from the registers may be made personally or by post. The agreed standard enquiries to accompany requisitions for official local land charges searches include questions asking for details of all entries on the registers affecting the land searched against.

Cost

Search of registers of applications and copy decisions, free. Search of Part III only of the local land charges register, varies between authorities.

Accommodation let

Information available

Where, prior to 15 January 1989, the rent for any premises has been fixed by a rent officer, or on appeal from him by a rent assessment committee, he enters particulars in a register kept by him. These include a brief specification of the premises, the rent payable (and whether it includes rates), the amount attributable to services, the parties to the tenancy when registered, and details of services and furniture (if any) provided by the landlord. Copies of entries can be obtained.

A similar register is maintained of market rents decided, after 15 January 1989, in respect of assured tenancies under the Housing Act 1988.

To whom available

Anyone may search.

How obtained

Personal application should be made to the rent officer for the area concerned for pre-1989 information, the local rent assessment panel for post-1989.

Cost

There is no search fee. Copy entry, £1 (rent officer); £1 (free to the parties), rent assessment panel.

Admissibility in evidence

A copy of an entry certified under the hand of the rent officer, or a person authorised by him, is evidence of that entry (Rent Act 1977, s 66(3)). For assured tenancies a copy certified by an officer duly authorised by the president of the rent assessment panel concerned is evidence of the entry (Housing Act 1988, s 42(2)).

Rent tribunal decisions

Information available

Particulars of any letting which has been the subject of a decision by a rent tribunal are given in a register maintained for this purpose. The details include the accommodation concerned (distinguishing between that occupied by the tenant alone and shared accommodation), whether furnished, and if so to what extent, what services are provided, the nature of any board supplied, the approved rent and the date of registration. Copies of the entries are available.

To whom available

Anyone may search, in person or by post.

How obtained

The register is maintained by the president of the rent assessment panel for the area. Postal searches may be made by using Oyez form Con 29E.

Cost

Postal search, £2.

Admissibility in evidence

A copy of an entry in the register certified under the hand of an officer duly authorised by the president of the rent assessment panel is evidence in any proceedings (Rent Act 1977, s 79(5), as amended by Housing Act 1980).

Houses in multiple occupation

Information available

Registers of houses in multiple occupation are maintained by local authorities. Each register is set up under a separate scheme, but details are similar in each case. Houses are registrable if they are occupied either by more than two households, or by one household and four persons. Information registered includes a description of the accommodation, the number of people living there and particulars of persons who receive rents and have any estate or interest in the premises.

To whom available

Anyone with an estate or interest in premises registered, or which appear to him to be registrable, may search in respect of those premises.

How obtained

Personal application should be made to the authority maintaining the register.

Cost

There is no fee.

Closed burial grounds

Information available

The Department of the Environment maintains a register of Orders in Council made to close particular burial grounds. The date of the order, date of closure and any exceptions to closure are recorded. Not all closed burial grounds are closed under this procedure and of the others the Department has no record. The majority of orders were made in the latter half of the 19th century, although a number continue to be made.

To whom available

Anyone may enquire.

How obtained

Enquiries may be made by letter or telephone to:

Room P1/117, Department of the Environment, 2 Marsham Street, London SW1P 3EB (Tel: 071–276 4052).

The burial ground should be identified as accurately as possible, and if it is a churchyard the patron saint of the church should be given.

Cost

There is no fee.

Places of public worship

Information available

The Registrar General maintains an official list of places of worship. This is divided into three sections: a list of churches in which marriages may lawfully be solemnised according to the rites of the Church of England and the Church in Wales; other denominations and religions; and naval, military and air force chapels. A list of those in the last two sections is published. The name and address of the certified places of worship are given, showing those registered for marriages and those for which authorised persons have been appointed. A certified copy of the record of a building's certification as a place of meeting for religious worship may be obtained. This shows the date on which the building was recorded in the General Register Office.

To whom available

Anyone may inspect (subject to prior appointment to inspect the original) and obtain certificates.

How obtained

The list is distributed to the offices of all superintendent registrars and registrars of births and deaths in England and Wales, where it may be inspected; it is also available at the General Register Office. Copies of the record of certification are obtained upon application by letter to:

The Registrar General, General Register Office, Smedley Hydro, Southport, Merseyside PR8 2HH (Tel: 051–471 4200).

Cost

Inspection of the list, and certified copy, free.

Other property

Motor vehicles

Licensing Centre

Information available

The name and address of the person in whose name a vehicle is registered may be obtained from the Driver and Vehicle Licensing Centre. The Centre can give other registered details about a vehicle, including the identity of the keeper on a particular date, details of the last licence issued and the number of previous keepers.

To whom available

The Centre will give information to registered keepers about their own vehicles, to official bodies such as the police and local authorities investigating an offence, and to other people who show reasonable cause for making their request.

How obtained

Application for information must be made by letter to:

Driver and Vehicle Licensing Centre, Enquiries from the Records Section, Oldway Centre, Swansea SA99 1AN (Tel: 0792 772134).

Cost

Enquiries by registered keepers, police and local authorities, free; others £3.50 per vehicle.

First registration

Information available

Motor vehicle licensing was originally carried out by county councils. When the licensee moved counties, the current records were transferred, but the information about the first registration of the vehicle was retained by the council responsible for that initial registration. When the licensing system was centralised, the current records were transferred to the Driver and Vehicle Licensing Centre, but some records about first registrations were transferred to county record offices.

To whom available

Anyone may search.

How obtained

Personal application should be made to the county record office.

It is possible to ascertain the date of first registration by telephone, from the Vehicle Check Services Line: 0839 858585. It is necessary to give registration number, make and model. NB that this is a (presently) 48p a minute service.

Cost

There is generally no fee.

Ships

Information available

For every British ship, except Her Majesty's ships and certain small ones, the statutory register book shows its name, port of registration, details in the surveyor's certificate (including tonnage and details of construction), origin, names and descriptions of its owners and the proportions in which they are interested. Mortgages in the statutory form are also registered. Returns of registered particulars are made by individual registrars to:

The Registrar General of Shipping and Seamen, Block 2,

Government Buildings, St Agnes Road, Gabalfa, Cardiff
CF4 4YA (Tel: 0222 586170).

Particulars of the ownership and construction of all known ocean-
going merchant ships of 100 tons and upwards are published in
Lloyd's Register Book (Lloyd's Register of Shipping).

To whom available

Anyone may inspect the statutory register.

How obtained

The register book of a British ship is kept by the Registrar of
Shipping at the port of registration. Copies may be obtained.
Lloyd's Register Book is published annually and weekly lists of
alterations and monthly cumulative supplements keep it up to
date. Non-subscribers may consult it personally at:

Lloyd's Register of Shipping, 71 Fenchurch Street, London
EC3M 4BS (Tel: 071–709 9166).

Cost

Search of statutory register, depends on work involved. Fee for
transcript, £26. Consultation of *Lloyd's Register Book* at the above
offices, free.

Admissibility in evidence

A copy or transcript of the register of British ships kept by the
Registrar General is admissible in all respects as the original
register (Merchant Shipping Act 1894, s 64(3)).

Trade marks

Information available

A search can be made to find whether a particular word or device
is registered as a trade mark in respect of any class of goods.
Records of trade marks up to 1938 have been transferred to the
Public Record Office.

Some trade marks are listed under the official classes, illustrated where necessary, with the owners' names, in *Trade Marks Journal* (Trade Marks Directory Service).

To whom available

Anyone may search. At the Public Record Office, a reader's ticket is required.

How obtained

A personal search is made in the classified indexes of trade marks at:

> Patent Office (Trade Marks Registry), 25 Southampton Buildings, London WC2A 1AY (Tel: 071–438 4700). Monday–Friday 10 am to 4 pm.

Goods are classified into thirty-four classes (fifty classes prior to 1938) and services into a further eight, and the searcher may see in which if any classes a word or device is registered. Entries relating to textile goods are also recorded at the Manchester Branch of the Registry, and entries relating to metal goods made in Hallamshire (Sheffield and a surrounding area) are kept by the Cutlers' Company in Sheffield. The old records may be inspected personally at:

> Public Record Office, Chancery Lane, London WC2A 1LR (Tel: 081–876 3444).

Three days' notice may be required for the production of records.

Cost

The fee varies depending on time taken and work involved. Including a standard £2 fee for copies, an average charge will be £5–10 per name per class.

Admissibility in evidence

Copy entries on the register certified by the Registrar, the Keeper of the Manchester Branch or the Master of the Cutlers' Company are admissible in all proceedings (Trade Marks Act 1938, ss 38, 39(11), 57(1), 58, Sched 2, para 13).

Patents

Information available

For all British patent applications the following particulars are entered on the register maintained at the Patent Office: name and address of the applicant, title of the invention, name and address of the inventor(s), date of the patent (if granted), and address for service. Assignments, transfers, mortgages and licences affecting patents may also be registered. Copies of specifications can be obtained. Enquiries may be addressed to the Comptroller as to whether a particular patent has expired. The register contains similar information about patents granted by the European Patent Office which are effective in the UK.

To whom available

Anyone may search and enquire.

How obtained

Searches are made in person at:

Patent Office, 25 Southampton Buildings, London WC2A 1AY (Tel: 071–438 4700). Monday–Friday 10 am to 4 pm.

Enquiries of the Comptroller should be addressed there. The patent number must be quoted.

Cost

There is no charge for a search. Copies are supplied at 24p plus VAT per page; if a whole patent is copied there is no VAT.

Admissibility in evidence

A copy of, or extract from, any entry on the register, document kept in the Patent Office or patent, certified by the Comptroller and under the seal of the Patent Office, is admissible without further proof, and is sufficient evidence in Scotland (Patents Act 1977, s 35(3)).

Registered designs

Information available

The names and addresses of the registered proprietors of registered designs may be obtained from the register, which also contains notices of assignments and transmissions. The representation or specimen of the design may be inspected and copies obtained. This is subject to the restriction that designs for textiles cannot be inspected for three years from the date of registration, and designs for wallpaper and lace not for two years, unless the searcher has the written authority of the registered proprietor. The Registrar will state, in reply to an enquiry identifying a design and furnishing the number, whether it is registered and if so in respect of what articles, the date of registration and the name of the registered proprietor. He will also state whether a given design applied to an article is identical to or closely resembles a subsisting registered design. Registers of designs up to 1910 have been transferred to the Public Record Office.

To whom available

With the restrictions upon the inspection of certain designs mentioned above, the information is available to all, except where a competent authority notifies the Registrar that it is relevant for defence purposes. Anyone with a reader's ticket may inspect the old records at the Public Record Office.

How obtained

The register is inspected personally at:

Designs Registry, 25 Southampton Buildings, London WC2A 1AY (Tel: 071–438 4700). Monday–Friday 10 am to 4 pm.

The information as to whether a certan design is registered is given in answer to a request on form Designs 20 if the enquirer has the registered number (although in that case it is cheaper merely to ask for a copy), or if not on form Designs 21. For these enquiries, a copy of the design in question must be supplied in duplicate. The old records may be inspected personally at:

Public Record Office, Ruskin Avenue, Kew, Richmond, Surrey TW9 4DN (Tel: 081–876 3444).

Cost

Inspection of the register, free. Copy entry, £3. Enquiries: on form Designs 20, free; on form Designs 21, £25. Public Record Office: no fee.

Admissibility in evidence

A copy entry or any representation, specimen or document certified by the Registrar and under the seal of the Patent Office is admissible in evidence (Registered Designs Act 1949, s 24(2)).

Copyright

Information available

The Stationers' Company has since 1924 maintained a register of books and fine arts voluntarily registered by copyright owners for purposes of record. The scope of the register includes maps, charts, music, circulars, patterns, photographs and engravings. Titles, authors and dates of registration are revealed on a search. On registration a copy of the work is deposited. The length of time for which copies will be retained is under review, and for the time being they are being kept indefinitely.

The statutory registers for the period 1842–1923 have been lodged with the Public Record Office.

To whom available

Anyone may ask for a search to be made. Requests to the Stationers' Company should be made in writing. A reader's ticket is required at the Public Record Office.

How obtained

Application is made to:

The Registrar, Stationers' Hall, Ave Maria Lane, London EC4M 7DD (Tel: 071–248 2934).

Certified copies of entries in the register can be obtained.

The statutory registers may be inspected on personal application to:

> Public Record Office, Ruskin Avenue, Kew, Richmond, Surrey TW9 4DN (Tel: 081–876 3444).

Cost

Stationers' Company search fee, £7 plus VAT; certified copy, £10 plus VAT. Public Record Office, no fee.

Newspapers

Information available

The Register of Newspaper Returns contains details relating to newspapers which are not owned by limited companies. The register gives the title of the newspaper and the names of all the proprietors with their respective occupations and places of business and residence. Returns are made annually in July and changes of ownership between annual returns are not necessarily recorded. For this purpose a 'newspaper' must be published at intervals not exceeding 26 days, and may contain only or principally advertisements. The entries in the register are arranged alphabetically under the names of the newspapers.

For general commercial information about all newspapers, see *Willing's Press Guide* (Reed Information Services).

For back issues, see p 132.

To whom available

Anyone may search.

How obtained

The register is kept at:

> Companies Registration Office, Companies House, Crown Way, Maindy, Cardiff CF4 3UZ (Tel: 0222 388588), and
>
> London Search Room, Companies House, 55–71 City Road,

London EC1Y 1BB (Tel: 081–253 9393). (Two days' notice required.)

A search should be made in person. Copies of returns are available.

Similar enquiries in Scotland and Northern Ireland should be made, respectively, to:

The Registrar of Companies, Exchequer Chambers, 102 George Street, Edinburgh EH2 2DJ (Tel: 031–225 5774).

The Registrar of Companies, IDB House, 43–47 Chichester Street, Belfast BT1 4RJ (Tel: 0232 234488).

Cost

Search, free. Copy return, 10p.

Admissibility in evidence

A copy of or an extract from the register certified by the registrar or his deputy, or under the official seal of the register, is admissible in all proceedings (Newspaper Libel and Registration Act 1881, s 15).

Commercial and professional

English and Scottish companies

Companies Registration Office

Information available

The information on any company's file may be divided into three classes: particulars of the constitution of the company, details of the persons in control of and interested in it, and financial information about it. The company's powers and regulations governing it are contained in its memorandum and articles of association, which are filed, as are any special resolutions amending them. They also define the company's capital structure, and the rights attaching to the different classes of shares. The date and details of any change of name are given.

On the allotment of shares, the names, addresses and occupations of shareholders are recorded, and each annual return contains an up-to-date list, also giving dates of acquiring and relinquishing shareholdings. The names, addresses, nationalities, business occupations and other directorships of all directors are given, together with their shareholdings and, for some companies, ages. The name and address of the secretary stated, as is the registered office. All changes are recorded as notified.

A balance sheet and profit and loss account are filed with the annual return. Auditors' and directors' reports are attached. For all companies the annual return gives a figure of secured indebtedness. Particulars of any mortgage or charge on any of the company's property, or any debenture, are given. These include the date of its creation, the amount secured, the property that forms the security and the name and address of the chargee. When a charge is repaid, a memorandum can be filed. On a voluntary liquidation, a declaration of solvency is filed (if appropriate) giving details of the company's financial position.

Where a company which has to file annual accounts has subsidiaries, group accounts must be filed, and the names of the subsidiaries will be revealed. In other cases, the names of associated companies may be apparent from the directors' other directorships.

Notices on the file record the appointment of a receiver on the enforcement of a security, or of a liquidator. In a voluntary liquidation, a copy of the resolution to wind up is filed. In a compulsory liquidation, an office copy of the court order is filed.

An overseas company which has not registered under Part XXIII of the Companies Act 1985 cannot register a charge over property, despite quoting an established place of business in England and Wales. See *NV Slavenburg's Bank* v *Intercontinental Natural Resources Ltd* [1980] 1 WLR 1076. Because of the inconvenience this causes, the Registrar maintains a non-statutory register of such companies known as the *Slavenburg* register.

How obtained

The file of the Registrar of Companies may be inspected in person or by post at:

Companies House, Crown Way, Maindy, Cardiff CF4 3UZ (Tel: 0222 388588).

Open Monday–Friday, 9 am to 5 pm.

It may also be inspected at:

London Search Room, Companies Registration Office, Companies House, 55–71 City Road, London EC1Y 1BB (Tel: 071–253 9393).

Open Monday–Friday, 9 am to 5 pm. Photographic copies of filed documents may be obtained.

The address of the Companies Registration Office in Scotland is:

Exchequer Chambers, 102 George Street, Edinburgh EH2 3DJ (Tel: 031–225 5774).

Microfilm information about Scottish companies may be ordered for inspection in Cardiff or London.

Cost

Search fee, £3 in person, £5.50 by post; *Slavenburg* register, free. Copy documents, 10p per sheet from a microfilm reader-printer, £7 per document by post. Certified copies of filed documents, 40p per page.

Admissibility in evidence

A copy of, or extract from, any filed document certified under the hand of the Registrar is equally admissible in evidence with the original document (Companies Act 1985, s 710). Returns by a company are prima facie admissible as evidence of the truth of the matters contained in them (*R v Halpin* (1975) *The Times*, 27 March).

Companies Court

Information available

Before an order is made on a winding-up or administration petition no record of the proceedings appears on the company's file at the Companies Registration Office. A register of petitions presented throughout the country to the High Court is, however, kept at the court.

How obtained

The High Court register is kept in:

> Room 209, Second Floor, Thomas More Building, Royal Courts of Justice, Strand, London WC2A 2LL (Tel: 071–936 7328 or 6294). Monday–Friday 10 am to 4.30 pm.

A search may be made in person and the database accessed. Alternatively, enquiries as to a maximum of three companies will be dealt with at the telephone. Two points should be mentioned: first, it is necessary specifically to request that the search include administration petitions; second, updating continues throughout the day and the search should be made as late as practicable.

Cost

No fee.

Companies not being compulsorily wound up

Information available

The name and address of the liquidator or receiver where the company is being wound up *other than compulsorily*. (This applies to about 90 per cent of liquidations.)

To whom available

Anyone may search.

How obtained

By telephone call to:

The Insolvency Service (Tel: 021–233 4808 extn 2311).

Cost

No charge is made.

Companies themselves

Information available

Every company must make available for inspection its register of charges and copies of instruments creating registered charges, its register of members and index of members' names (if any), and the register of its directors and secretaries, giving their names and addresses and the other directorships of directors. The register of members will often be more accurate than the list filed at the Companies Registration Office, because the latter is not amended between annual returns. Copies of the register of members may be obtained.

A public company may require anyone known or believed to be, or within the last three years to have been, interested in its shares to supply details. This power can be exercised to reveal the identity of the beneficial ownership of shares held by nominees. The fact that a requirement was made and the information received in response is registered by the company. Entries recording that the person had ceased to be interested in any of the company's shares, and those superseded by later entries relating to the same person, may be removed from the register after six years.

To whom available

Anyone may inspect the registers and index. The copy instruments of charge are only open to members and creditors of the company.

How obtained

Application should be made to the company at its registered office, or such other place at which its annual return shows the statutory books are kept.

Cost

Inspection of register of members: members and (for instruments of charge and the charges register) creditors, free; others, any fee fixed by the company, maximum 5p. Inspection of register of interests, free. Copies of the registers, as fixed by the company, maximum 10p per 100 words.

Admissibility in evidence

The register of members is prima facie evidence of the facts authorised to be recorded in it (Companies Act 1985, s 361).

Reference books

Information available

Many reference books, published regularly, give information about public companies. A summary of capitalisation, share structure and registration details for all quoted companies appears in *The Stock Exchange Official Year Book* (Macmillan). The relationship of companies in groups is given in *Who Owns Whom (UK Edition)* (Dun & Bradstreet). Names, and some addresses, of directors with their directorships appear in *The Directory of Directors* (Reed Information Services).

Defunct companies

Information available

Some files of dissolved companies have been transferred from the
Companies Registration Office to the Public Record Office. These
are generally, first, those struck off the register by the Registrar
as defunct prior to 1933, and those voluntarily dissolved before
1948. Before removal four out of five of the annual returns in 99
out of 100 of those files were destroyed, although any accounts
and reports filed with the returns were kept. Second, the files of
all companies dissolved before 1972—however, before transfer,
nine out of ten annual returns from the files of non-exempt private
companies were destroyed (except accounts and reports
accompanying them), and 99 out of 100 files of the former exempt
private companies were destroyed completely. Brief details of the
companies whose files have been destroyed are recorded by the
Registrar of Companies.

The files of all companies dissolved since 1964 are stored in Cardiff.
A card index of companies dissolved earlier is available only at
Companies House in London.

To whom available

Anyone may search, but at the Public Record Office a reader's
ticket is required.

How obtained

Personal application must be made at the appropriate offices:

Companies Registration Office, Crown Way, Maindy, Cardiff
(Tel: 0222 388588). (24 hours' notice may be required.)

Companies House, 55–71 City Road, London EC1Y 1BB
(Tel: 071–253 9393). (Longer notice may be needed here.)

Public Record Office, Ruskin Avenue, Kew, Richmond,
Surrey TW9 4DU (Tel: 081–876 3444).

Copies of documents still on the file may be obtained. The Registrar
of Companies keeps a record of all dissolved companies and in

response to a letter will give the whereabouts of a particular file, and a Public Record Office reference if appropriate. Telephone enquiries may be made to 0222 380801.

Cost

Companies Registration Office, search fee, £6 for dissolutions 1972–6, otherwise £3. Public Record Office, no fee.

Northern Ireland companies

Information available

The information registered in relation to Northern Ireland companies is the same as that in respect of English companies, except that private company accounts did not have to be filed before 1 July 1983.

To whom available

Anyone may search.

How obtained

Files must be inspected personally at:

Companies Registry, 43–47 Chichester St, Belfast BT1 4RJ (Tel: 0232 234488).

The search room is open Monday–Friday, 10 am to 1 pm and 2 pm to 4 pm.

Cost

Search fee, £1. Copy documents, 10p per sheet.

Jersey companies

Information available

The only details which a Jersey company is required to register are: its nominal and issued capital, registered office and shareholders. It does not have to register particulars of its directors or secretary, although annual returns have to be signed by directors or a director and secretary and the names may be available from that source.

To whom available

Anyone may search.

How obtained

Personal, postal or fax application may be made to:

The Financial Services Department, Cyril le Marquand House, PO Box 267, The Parade, St Helier, Jersey JE4 8TZ (Tel: 0534 603614/6; Fax: 0534 603610).

Other Channel Islands companies registration departments are:

Guernsey The Greffier, Royal Court House, St Peter Port, Guernsey.

Alderney Clerk of the Court, States Office, New St, Alderney.

Cost

Search: personal £3; postal £6. Copies 25p per page, certification £10. Certificate of good standing £10. All fees to be paid with application.

Isle of Man companies

Information available

The registered information is similar to that registered at the Companies Registration Office for English companies, with the following principal exceptions. The financial information required from private companies, which most Manx companies are, is limited to details of the authorised and issued share capital. A director without a business occupation need only give details of another directorship, and directors' ages are never given. A declaration of solvency on a voluntary liquidation does not give details of the company's financial position.

To whom available

Anyone can search.

How obtained

Application should be made by post or fax to:

> The Chief Registrar, General Registry, Finch Road, Douglas, Isle of Man (Tel: 0624 685233; Fax: 0624 685236).

Cost

Copies, £2 plus 15p per page. Certification, £2 plus 15p per page. By fax: £14 plus 15p a page.

Foreign companies

Carrying on business in England

Information available

Companies incorporated abroad, ie outside Great Britain, establishing a place of business in England must file with the Registrar of Companies a copy of the constitution of the company (with a translation if necessary). The following additional particulars must be given: the names, address, nationality, business occupation or other directorships of each director, the names and address of the secretary, a name and address for service in Great Britain, and annual accounts. This information must be kept up to date. Files closed because the companies have been dissolved or are no longer required to register are retained by the Registrar.

The names of companies which have not registered but have nevertheless recorded a regular place of business in England and Wales in connection with a charge are recorded on the non-statutory *Slavenburg* register.

To whom available

Anyone may inspect.

How obtained

Applications to search files must be made in person at:

Companies Registration Office, Crown Way, Maindy, Cardiff (Tel: 0222 388588), and

London Search Room, Companies House, 55–71 City Road, London EC1Y 1BB (Tel: 071–253 9393).

Cost

Search fee, £3; *Slavenburg* register, free.

European companies

Details of sources of information about companies in Europe— both official and in commercial directories—are given in *European Companies: A Guide to Sources of Information* (CBD Research Ltd). This also gives for each country a glossary of terms used in the headings of native language reference books to enable English speakers to use them.

Disqualified directors

Information available

The Registrar of Companies maintains a list of the names of people who have been disqualified by court order from acting as directors of companies.

To whom available

Anyone may search.

How obtained

Personal application should be made to:

Companies Registration Office, Crown Way, Maindy, Cardiff CF4 3UZ (Tel: 0222 388588), and

London Search Room, Companies House, 55–71 City Road, London EC1Y 1BB (Tel: 071–253 9393).

Cost

Inspection, free. Copies: £10 for the complete list, 10p a page photocopies.

Business names

Information available

Anyone carrying on business under a name other than an exempt name must comply with certain disclosure rules. Exempt names are: in the case of an individual his surname with or without his forename or initial; in the case of a partnership the surname or corporate name of all partners, adding 's' if required where more than one partner has the same name; in the case of a company its corporate name. The names of the principal or each partner, and an address for service in Great Britain for each person named, must be prominently displayed in any premises where the business is carried on and to which customers or suppliers have access. They must also be disclosed in writing to anyone with whom anything is done or discussed in the course of the business and who so requests. A partnership of more than 20 members may maintain a list of partners at its principal place of business instead of complying with disclosure requirements on documents. That list has to be available for inspection during office hours.

To whom available

Any lawful caller at the business' premises may inspect the information displayed. A person who qualifies by dealing with the business may require information in writing. The list maintained by large partnerships must be made available to any person.

How obtained

Personal attendance at the office of the business is necessary, except for those who qualify for written information who may request it in any convenient way.

Cost

No fee may be charged. Refusal of information without reasonable excuse can be an offence (Companies Act 1981, s 29).

Limited partnerships

Limited partnerships must file the following particulars and keep them up to date: the firm's name, the general nature of its business, its principal place of business, the term (if any) of the partnership and when it commenced. Each partner must be named, and the limited partners described as such with a note of the sum contributed by each, stating whether in cash or otherwise.

Similar information for limited partnerships registered in Scotland and Northern Ireland is available from:

Scotland Registrar of Limited Partnerships, 102 George St, Edinburgh EH2 3DJ (Tel: 031–225 5774).

Northern Ireland Registrar of Limited Partnerships, IBD House, 43–47 Chichester St, Belfast BT1 4RJ (Tel: 0232 234488).

To whom available

Anyone may search.

How obtained

The register is kept by the Registrar of Limited Partnerships, and may be inspected at:

Companies Registration Office, Crown Way, Maindy, Cardiff (Tel: 0222 388588).

Copies can be made available on two days' notice at:

London Search Room, Companies House, 55–71 City Road, London EC1Y 1BB (Tel: 071–253 9393).

Applications to search should be made in person.

Cost

Search fee, £3. Copies, 10p per page.

Insurance companies

Information available

The names and addresses of members and the deed of settlement of insurers carrying on business in Great Britain, with major exceptions, must be made available. This does not apply to those registered as companies or friendly societies, nor to Lloyd's underwriters, trade unions or employers' associations.

To whom available

Shareholders and policy holders may apply.

How obtained

Application is made direct to the insurers.

Cost

The maximum fees chargeable are: copies of shareholders' address book, 2½p per 100 words, copy deed of settlement, 5p.

Housing associations

Information available

The Housing Corporation maintains the register of housing associations registered under the Housing Act 1974 (as amended). The register, and an index with it, gives for each association: its registered office, address for correspondence, type(s) of dwelling provided, brief particulars of its governing instrument and (where applicable) registered numbers allotted by the Registrar of Friendly Societies and the Charity Commissioners. A separate register file for each association contains a copy of the governing instrument and copies of the last three years' accounts and annual returns. Copies of register entries and filed documents may be obtained.

To whom available

Anyone may search.

How obtained

Searches may be made by personal application and telephone, and will probably be answered by post. Regional offices of the Corporation have details of associations in their areas, but the separate register file is available only with the register itself at:

Housing Corporation, Registration and Supervision Division, 149 Tottenham Court Rd, London W1P 0BN (Tel: 071-387 9466).

The regional offices and their areas of responsibility are:

London and Home Counties (South) Leon House, High Street, Croydon CR9 1UH (Tel: 081-681 3771).

London and Home Counties (North) Waverley House, 7-12 Noel Street, London W1V 4BA (Tel: North East — 071-434 0026; North West—071-434 2162).

West 2nd Floor Beaufort House, 51 New North Road, Exeter EX4 4EP (Tel: 0392 50152).

East Midlands Attenborough House, 109/119 Charles Street, Leicester LE1 1FQ (Tel: 0533 623600).

West Midlands Norwich Union House, Waterloo Road, Wolverhampton WV1 4BP (Tel: 0902 24654).

North East St Pauls House, 23 Park Square South, Leeds LS1 2ND (Tel: 0532 469601).

Merseyside 6th floor, Corn Exchange Buildings, Fenwick Street, Liverpool L2 7RD (Tel: 051-236 0406).

North West Elisabeth House, 16 St Peters Square, Manchester M2 3DF (Tel: 061-228 2951).

Housing for Wales (Tai Cymru) 25-30 Lambourne Crescent, Llanishen, Cardiff CF4 5ZJ (Tel: 0222 747979).

Scottish Homes Thistle House, 91 Haymarket Terrace, Edinburgh EH12 5HE (Tel: 031-313 0044).

Cost

Inspection of the index, no fee. Inspection of the register, £3. Inspection of a register file, £3 for one to five files, £5 for six to ten files, thereafter £1 per file. Copy or extract of any document on a register file, 20p a page, minimum £2, plus £1 p&p. For any signed certificate of authenticity, an additional £15. In addition, copies of the whole register may be purchased (the 1992 register cost £16).

Building societies

Information available

The rules of each society are registered and open for inspection, together with a notice of the address of the chief office for the time being, notices of changes of name and transfers of engagements. Since 1960 the names of the directors and manager or secretary have been given, and since 1986 all statutory documents have been available. Annual returns and statements of accounts are filed. Orders restricting the receipt of share contributions or deposits, with the reasons for making them, may be inspected, as may orders restricting advertising. Copies of the filed documents may be obtained.

Details of building societies are published annually in *Building Societies Year Book* (Franey & Co Ltd). Head office addresses are listed in the *Longman Directory of Local Authorities* (Longman Group UK Ltd) and *Whitaker's Almanac* (J Whitaker & Sons Ltd).

To whom available

Anyone may search.

How obtained

Application should be made in person (subject to making an appointment) or by post to:

Building Societies Commission, 15 Great Marlborough Street, London W1V 2AX (Tel: 071–437 9992).

Cost

Search fee, £4. Copies, 25p per sheet, plus £5 postage and packing.

Friendly societies

Information available

The following details are available from the register for each friendly society registered under the Friendly Societies Acts: rules; notice of the registered office for the time being; notice of any change of name; names of trustees, or officer authorised to sue and be sued; names of committee of management and secretary for collecting (industrial assurance) societies; annual returns and audited accounts made up to 31 December; actuarial valuations of assets and liabilities (which must be at least quinquennial); special resolutions; and any instrument or award of dissolution or winding-up order. If a branch has funds under its own control it is registered separately. Other bodies are registrable under the same Acts: cattle insurance societies, benevolent societies, working men's clubs, old people's homes societies and other specially authorised societies. (The latter are a miscellaneous collection most devoted to some form of worthy cause.) The information for these is as nearly as possible the same as for friendly societies. Copies of filed documents can be obtained.

To whom available

Anyone may search.

How obtained

Application in person (subject to making an appointment) or by post is made to:

The Chief Registrar of Friendly Societies, 15 Great Marlborough Street, London W1V 2AX (Tel: 071-437 9992). (0171) 463 5000

The equivalent information for Scotland and Northern Ireland is kept at the following addresses:

58 Frederick Street, Edinburgh EH2 1AB (Tel: 031-226 3224), and

IBD House, 64 Chichester Street, Belfast BT1 4JX (Tel: 0232 234488).

Cost

Search fee, £4. Copies, 25p per sheet, plus £5 postage and packing.

Admissibility in evidence

Any printed document purporting to be a copy of the rules or memorandum of a friendly society or registered branch and certified by the secretary or other officer of the society or branch, and any other document signed by a registrar on behalf of the Central Office, shall—in the absence of evidence to the contrary—be deemed to be such a copy or to have been so signed (Friendly Societies Act 1992, s 111).

Industrial and provident societies

Information available

Societies incorporated under the Industrial and Provident Societies Acts vary considerably in scope and include co-operative societies, clubs, banks, insurance and superannuation societies and housing associations, although not all organisations in those categories come within the scope of these Acts. The information available varies with the type of organisation, but usually includes: rules, note of registered office for the time being and annual return with summary of accounts. If a floating charge on agricultural equipment is made in favour of a bank which is registered as an agricultural credit (p 42), a notice is recorded on the society's file. Copies of filed documents may be obtained.

To whom available

Anyone may search.

How obtained

Application may be made in person (subject to prior appointment) or by letter to:

The Chief Registrar of Industrial and Provident Societies, 15 Great Marlborough Street, London W1V 2AX ~~(Tel: 071–437 9992).~~ (0171) 663 5000

Certain details of societies registered in Scotland and Northern Ireland are recorded in London if the society operates in England.

Cost

Search fee, £4. Copies 60 ~~25~~p per sheet, plus £5 postage and packing.

Certified loan societies

Information available

The rules, names and addresses of trustees, secretary and auditors, and accounts may be inspected.

To whom available

Anyone may search.

How obtained

Application may be made in person or by post to:

The Chief Registrar of Friendly Societies, 15 Great Marlborough Street, London W1V 2AX (Tel: 071–437 9992).

Cost

No fee.

Credit traders

Information available

Various businesses offering or dealing with credit for consumers are required to have licences under the Consumer Credit Act 1974. They are businesses in the following fields: consumer credit, consumer hire, credit brokerage, debt adjusting and debt counselling, debt collecting, and credit reference agencies. There is an

index of applicants and licensees by true name and by business
name, and a file for each applicant.

To whom available

Anyone may search.

How obtained

The register is maintained by:

Office of Fair Trading, Government Building, Bromyard
Avenue, Acton, London W3 7BB (Tel: 071–269 8616).

Personal searches can be conducted between 10 am and 4 pm,
Monday–Friday (public holidays excluded). Copies of documents
which are clearly identified can be obtained by post.

Cost

Inspection: names index, free; files, £3.50 each. Copies on personal application: uncertified, £1 per sheet; certified, £2 per
sheedt. Copies by post: uncertified copy licence, £1; certified copy
licence, £3; plus handling fee and postage £2.50.

Restrictive trading agreements

Information available

Indexes list registered agreements under their names and under
commodities and services dealt with, and show if they are confined
to a particular area. The files contain the terms of the agreement
concerned, and notices of any court hearing and orders made.
Copies can be obtained.

To whom available

Anyone may search, in person or by post.

How obtained

The public register is kept at:

Office of Fair Trading, Room 404D, Government Building,
Bromyard Avenue, Acton, London W3 7BB.

It is open for inspection from 10 am to 4.30 pm, Monday–Friday (excluding public holidays). Copies of agreements or extracts, certified by the Director General as true copies or extracts, are available by post.

Cost

Search fee, £1 per agreement, maximum £10 a day. Copies, 35p per sheet.

Admissibility in evidence

A copy of, or extract from, any document entered or filed in the register certified by the Director General is admissible in evidence and of equal validity with the original (Restrictive Trade Practices Act 1976, s 23(7)).

Solicitors

Information available

The roll of solicitors consists of an alphabetical list of the names of all solicitors. The roll, or a copy of it when it is kept by computer, is available for inspection. There are also registers of practising solicitors, giving the names of all solicitors practising in England and Wales, and of incorporated practices, giving the names and business addresses of all recognised bodies corporate providing legal services.

To whom available

Anyone may inspect.

How obtained

Application should be made during office hours to:

The Law Society, 113 Chancery Lane, London WC2A 1PL (Tel: 071–242 1222).

Cost

There is no search fee.

Admissibility in evidence

In the case of a person not named, an extract from the roll certified by the Law Society is evidence of the facts in the extract (Solicitors Act 1974, s 18).

Licensed conveyancers

Information available

The name and place(s) of business of all persons holding a licence. Where any licence is suspended, the fact is available, and details of any conditions.

To whom available

Anyone may search.

How obtained

Application may be made in person, by post or by telephone to:

Council for Licensed Conveyancers, Suite 4 Cairngorm House, 203 Marsh Wall, Docklands, London E14 9YT (Tel: 071–537 2953).

Cost

No charge for specific enquiries. There is a full list of licensed conveyancers, updated regularly, and a copy of this will cost £15.

Admissibility in evidence

A certificate signed by an officer of the Council that a person does or does not, or did or did not, hold a licence at any time, or that any such licence was free of—or subject to any particular—conditions, is evidence of those facts unless the contrary is proved. A certificate purporting to be so signed is to be taken as so signed unless the contrary be proved (Administration of Justice Act 1985, s 19(5)).

Auditors

Information available

Each of the five recognised supervisory bodies (see below) is required to keep a register of individuals, firms and companies eligible to be appointed as auditor to a company. For companies the register must contain the names and addresses of all directors and members, for firms the name and address of every partner, and the names and addresses of individuals. Telephone and fax numbers are given, and the date of registration.

To whom available

Anyone may search.

How obtained

Each of the five bodies maintains its own register. Updates are submitted weekly to the ICAS, which combines all the registers on to one database and provides each of the others with a complete update. All registers may therefore be inspected in person or by telephone at:

Institute of Chartered Accountants in England and Wales (ICAEW), Chartered Accountants Hall, Moorgate Place, London EC2P 2BJ (Tel: 071–920 8100).

Institute of Chartered Accountants of Scotland (ICAS), 27 Queen Street, Edinburgh EH2 1LA (Tel: 031–225 5673).

Institute of Chartered Accountants in Ireland (ICAI), 11 Donegal Square South, Belfast BT1 5JE (Tel: 0232 321600).

Chartered Accountants House, 87–89 Pembroke Road, Ballsbridge, Dublin 4 (Tel: 010 353 1 680400).

Chartered Association of Certified Accountants (ACCA), 29 Lincoln's Inn Fields, London WC2A 3EE (Tel: 071–242 6855).

Association of Authorised Public Accountants (AAPA), 10 Cornfield Road, Eastbourne, East Sussex BN21 4QE (Tel: 0323 410412).

Cost

Basically free of charge, but a charge may be made if a substantial enquiry is made and a number of copies or print-outs taken.

Financial services

Information available

The name or trading name, address and telephone number of every authorised investment firm's main place of business, its SIB registration number, and a statement and date of its authorisation status. The Self-Regulating Organisation (FIMBRA, IMRO, LAUTRO or SFA) or Recognised Professional Body (ACCA, ICAEW, ICAI, ICAS, IBRC, Institute of Actuaries, the Law Societies of England, Northern Ireland and Scotland) by which the firm is regulated (or, if that be the case, the SIB itself) is also identified. The entry will state whether the firm may handle clients' money and the types of investment business the firm is permitted to engage in. Finally, there will be a note of any warning messages: whether, for example, the firm is in liquidation or is subject to any disciplinary action, such as suspension.

To whom available

Anyone may search.

How obtained

In person, by post or by telephone to:

Securities and Investments Board (SIB), Gavrelle House, 2–14 Bunhill Row, London EC1Y 8RA (Tel: 071–929 3652).

Alternatively, the register may be accessed via Prestel (*SIB# or *301#) or, for professional users, via BTIS or Telecom Gold.

Cost

Free of charge (other than, of course, on-line charges for Prestel etc).

Doctors

Information available

The register lists all registered medical practitioners who are currently registered, giving their full names, address, sex, qualifications, date of initial registration and registration number. This information, together if appropriate with the date that the name was erased from the register, on death or otherwise, is available in respect of doctors now or formerly registered.

The Medical Register (General Medical Council), published annually lists doctors fully or provisionally registered in the Principal List of the register on 1 January of the year of publication. It is a three-volume publication, and the 1993 edition costs £90.

To whom available

Anyone may enquire.

How obtained

Enquiries, giving all known details, should be addressed to:

General Medical Council, 44 Hallam Street, London W1N 6AE (Tel: 071–580 7642).

Cost

Fewer than five names, the information will be provided at the telephone, without charge. For more names, a fee will be charged based on the work involved.

Dentists

Information available

The register of dentists lists all registered dentists, giving their full names, a registered address, their date of qualification and registration number.

To whom available

Anyone may enquire.

How obtained

Copies are usually available in libraries. Otherwise, enquiries should be made of:

General Dental Council, 37 Wimpole Street, London W1M 8DQ (Tel: 071–486 2171). Open to the public 9.15 am to 4 pm Monday—Friday.

Cost

Enquiries, free. A copy of the whole list may be purchased: the 1992 one costs £15.50, earlier ones less. Copies of individual pages may be obtained from libraries.

Admissibility in evidence

A certificate under the hand of the registrar to the effect that a person was, or was not, entered on the register at a particular date, and as to the details of an entry on the register is prima facie evidence of the facts stated (Dentists Act 1984, s 14(6)).

Opticians

Information available

Name, qualification and practice address of all registered opticians. The register has five sections: optometrists (who both test and fit and supply); those who test only; those who fit and supply only; companies; and dispensing opticians.

To whom available

Anyone may search.

How obtained

Copies of the register are available at local libraries. Otherwise, apply to:

General Optical Council, 41 Harley Street, London W1N
2DJ (Tel: 071–580 3898).

Cost

Inspection at local library free. A copy of the entire register may
be purchased from the Council at a cost (for the 1993 register) of
£25 plus £2.50 postage and packing.

Estate agents

Information available

Under the Estate Agents Act 1979, the Director General of Fair
Trading can make a warning order or a prohibition order against
an estate agent covered by the Act. He maintains a register of
those orders, including variations and revocations of them, and
details of any pending appeals against them. There is an index of
the names of persons appearing on the register.

To whom available

Anyone may search.

How obtained

The register is kept at:

Office of Fair Trading, Government Building, Bromyard
Avenue, Acton, London W3 7BB (Tel: 071–269 8640).

From 10 am to 4 pm, Monday–Friday (other than public holidays),
personal callers may inspect the index of names and the file
entries. Copies of clearly identified documents, certified as true
copies by the Director General, will be supplied by post.

Cost

Inspection: index, free; file entries, per file: £1 uncertified, £2
certified.

Admissibility in evidence

A copy of an entry on the register certified by the Director General to be correct is conclusive evidence that on the date of the certificate the particulars in the copy were entered on the register (Estate Agents Act 1979, s 8(6)).

Agricultural experts and witnesses

Information available

Names and addresses of experts in matters agricultural, horticultural, etc, and on questions of amenity, rural planning and the like.

To whom available

Anyone may apply.

How obtained

Apply by telephone to:

H. J. Nation, Secretary, British Institute of Agricultural Consultants, Wrest Park, Silsoe, Bedfordshire MK45 4HS (Tel: 0525 860000 extn 2595).

Copies of the lists of experts and those prepared to act as expert witnesses will be furnished.

Cost

Free of charge.

Sports

Information available

Lists of sporting events for the year are published annually and past issues are available. There are also lists giving the name, address and telephone number of all the governing bodies of sport and the name, address and telephone number of all sports centres.

To whom available

Anyone may apply.

How obtained

Apply in writing, with a stamped, addressed envelope, to:

The Sports Council, 16 Upper Woburn Place, London WC1H 0QP (Tel: 071–388 1277).

Cost

In addition to the SAE, the list of sports centres costs £5 (payable with request) but the other lists are free. If a quantity of back issues of the events list is requested, a copying charge may be made.

Professions

Information available

Many professional bodies publish lists of their members. Some lists are also published commercially, sometimes under the auspices of the professional bodies concerned. While the content of these lists varies, they generally contain the names of practitioners, the names of firms and the addresses from which they practise. The following books, many revised annually, may be referred to:

Accountants. *The Institute of Chartered Accountants in England and Wales — List of Members*; *List of Members — Association of Certified Accountants*; *Official Directory — Institute of Chartered Accountants of Scotland*; *List of Members — ICAI*.

Actuaries. *List of Members*.

Architects. *Register of Architects* (Architects Registration Council of United Kingdom); *RIBA Directory of Practices* (Royal Institute of British Architects).

Clergymen. *Catholic Directory of England and Wales* (Gabriel Books); *Crockford's Clerical Directory* (Church House Publishing).

Dentists. *The Dentists Register* (General Dental Council).

Doctors. *The Medical Directory* (Churchill Livingstone); *The Medical Register* (General Medical Council).

Lawyers. *Solicitors and Barristers Directory* (Waterlow Information Services); *Scottish Law List* (T & T Clark); *The Directory* (Northern Ireland Law Society); *Law Directory and Diary* (Incorporated Law Society of Ireland).

Opticians. *Opticians Register* (General Optical Council).

Secretaries. *Institute of Chartered Secretaries and Administrators — List of Members.*

Stockbrokers. *Member Firms of the Stock Exchange* (The Council of the Stock Exchange).

Surveyors, etc. *The Chartered Auctioneers and Estate Agents' Year Book and List of Members*; *The Incorporated Society of Auctioneers and Landed Property Agents — List of Members*; *Incorporated Society of Valuers and Auctioneers — List of Members and Firms*; *The Royal Institution of Chartered Surveyors' Year Book* (Macmillan/RICS).

Bookmakers

Information available

Bookmakers' permits The register contains the name and last known address of the holder of each permit and, if the holder is a company, of its directors, and names of any persons in accordance with whose instructions they are accustomed to act. The dates of renewal and expiry of the permit are also given.

Betting agency permits To the information given for the bookmakers' permits there is added the name and address of the person by whom the agent is accredited.

Betting offices The name, address and description of the licensee is given with the address of the premises. Particulars are also given of the bookmakers' or betting agency permit held by the licensee.

To whom available

Anyone may search.

How obtained

Personal application should be made to the clerk to the Betting Licensing Committee.

Cost

Search fee, 5p (but some do not charge). Police officers, free.

Residential homes

Information available

Residential homes offering accommodation for disabled people, old people or those suffering from mental disorder, whether or not for reward, are registered with the social services department of the local authority. The registration states the person authorised to carry on the home, and may impose conditions as to the number, age, sex or other category of people to be accommodated there. Establishments intending to accommodate fewer than four persons need not register, neither need certain specified establishments such as hospitals, universities, etc.

To whom available

Anyone may search.

How obtained

Personal application should be made to the authority in whose area the home is.

Cost

Inspection free. Copies made by the person inspecting, as fixed by the authority.

Nurseries and child-minders

Information available

Registers are maintained by local social services authorities of premises in their areas where children under the minimum school leaving age are looked after. Private houses, schools and hospitals are not included. A further register lists persons who look after children under five in their own houses for reward.

To whom available

Anyone may inspect the register.

How obtained

Personal application should be made to the local authority offices.

Cost

There is no inspection fee.

Miscellaneous

Charities

Information available

The Charity Commissioners keep a register of all charities registered with them. Copies of the Commissioners' index slips have been made available for local registers to be compiled (see below). The public information about the charities which have already been registered is indexed so that it may be referred to in any of three ways: by the name of the charity, by the nature of its objects, or by the area intended to be benefited. In each case the information available is: the name of the charity, particulars of its governing instrument, its objects, its beneficial area, its approximate annual income (if known), and the name and address of its correspondent. The latter may be its secretary or other official, one of its trustees, or some professional firm that deals with queries on its behalf. A copy of the charity's annual accounts may also be inspected if available. The entries cancelled when institutions are removed from the register are also available. The deeds forming part of the register may be inspected at the Charity Commission offices, on giving prior notice.

Details of many major charities are given in the annual *Charities Digest* (Family Welfare Association), and particulars of many trusts making grants are published in *Directory of Grant Making Trusts* (Charities Aid Foundation).

To whom available

Anyone may search.

How obtained

Personal application must be made at the following addresses:

Central register

Charity Commission (Registration Division), St Albans House, 57–60 Haymarket, London SW1Y 4QX (Tel: 071–210 4477).

Charity Commission (Registration Division), Graeme House, Derby Square, Liverpool L2 7SB (Tel: 051–227 3191).

Local indexes of national charities

Bristol   Avon County Central Library, The Council House, College Green, Bristol BS1 5TL (Tel: 0272 261121).

Caerphilly   Wales Council for Voluntary Action, Crescent Road, Caerphilly, Mid Glamorgan CF8 1XL (Tel: 0222 869111).

Manchester   Manchester City Council, Town Hall, Manchester M60 2LA (Tel: 061–234 5000).

Morpeth   Northumberland County Council, County Hall, Morpeth, Northumberland NE61 2EF (Tel: 0670 533000).

Tonbridge   Charities Aid Foundation, 48 Pembury Road, Tonbridge, Kent TN9 2JD (Tel: 0732 771333).

York   York Central Library, Museum Street, York YO1 2DS (Tel: 0904 655631).

Local indexes of local charities

The offices of the county, London borough, borough or district council for the area.

Cost

No search fee. The Charity Commission will charge for any copy document supplied. Even copy documents ordered by personal searchers have to be forwarded by post.

Data protection

Information available

The names and addresses of data users who hold (and bureaux that provide services in respect of) personal data; in respect of users, details of the data and the purposes for which it is held, a description of the source(s) of the data, names of any countries outside the UK to which the data may be transmitted, and one or more addresses for the receipt of requests from data subjects (see below).

To whom available

Anyone may search.

How obtained

Apply by post or telephone to:

Office of the Data Protection Registrar, Wycliffe House, Water Lane, Wilmslow, Cheshire SK9 5AF (Tel: 0625 535711).

Cost

Search and print-out of an entry, free. Certified copy £2.

Protection of data subjects

Any person may apply in writing to a data user to be informed whether data held by the user include personal data relating to the applicant, and for a copy of any such data. The user may (but is not obliged to) charge a prescribed fee (current maximum £10) for the service, and a separate fee may be charged for separate entries in respect of data held for different purposes. The data user is entitled to satisfy himself as to the applicant's identity, and has to comply with the request within 40 days.

Licensed premises

Information available

All premises in respect of which justices' licences have been issued for the sale of intoxicating liquor (both on-licences and off-licences) are recorded on a register for each district. This gives the names of the owners and licensees of each premises. Notices of convictions of holders of justices' licences for offences committed by them as such, forfeitures of licences and disqualifications of premises are also recorded.

To whom available

Only the following may inspect the register: ratepayers for that district, owners of licensed premises and holders of justices' licences in the district, and police and customs and excise officers.

How obtained

The register is kept by the clerk to the licensing justices, to whom personal application should be made.

Cost

Search fee, 5p (often not charged), except that no fee is payable by police or customs and excise officers.

Admissibility in evidence

The register, and any copy entry in it certified by the clerk to the licensing justices, may be received in evidence (Licensing Act 1964, s 30(4)).

Licensing applications

Information available

A list of persons who have given notice to apply for justices' licences, with their addresses, the nature of the application and address of the premises concerned (but not plans), is available for each licensing session.

To whom available

Anyone may inspect the list.

How obtained

Application must be made in person to the clerk to the licensing justices during the 14 days preceding the sessions.

Cost

Inspection fee, 5p (often not charged); free to customs and excise officers.

Registered clubs

Information available

A register is kept of those clubs registered for the supply of alcoholic liquor. This shows the name of the club, its secretary and its objects, the premises registered and the hours of service of liquor. The date of issue or renewal of the certificate of registration and its period of validity are also shown.

To whom available

Anyone may inspect the register.

How obtained

Personal application should be made to the clerk to the justices for the district concerned.

Cost

Search fee 5p (often not charged), but free to a police or customs and excise officer or an officer of a local authority authorised in writing to inspect the register on its behalf.

High Court litigation

Information available

The following documents, filed in the Central Office of the Supreme Court or in district registries, are freely available: copies of writs of summons or other originating process, judgments or orders given or made in court. Any other document is available with leave of the court. Application is made ex parte.

Many court records are transferred to the Public Record Office after a period. The practice varies with the type of document, but chancery orders, for instance, will usually be transferred about twenty-five years after they are made.

(See also Divorce, p 17; Bankruptcy, p 39; Companies Court, p 92.)

To whom available

With the restrictions noted in the previous paragraph, the information is available to all. At the Public Record Office, a reader's ticket is required.

How obtained

For records still retained by the court, application should be made in person to the office holding the particular records. The officials in charge may insist that the searcher obtain leave. Application should be made in person to:

Public Record Office, Chancery Lane, London WC2A 1LR (Tel: 081–876 3444).

Some notice may be needed before records are produced.

Cost

Search fee: Central Office, £1; Public Record office, no fee. Copies from the court: 25p per page photographic, 50p per page typed. Copies for production in evidence sent by post: £1 first document, thereafter 25p per document. Copies from the Public Record Office: cost according to size and method of reproduction.

Admissibility in evidence

Office copies are admissible in evidence in any proceedings, between any parties, to the same extent as the originals (RSC, Ord 38, r 10).

Documents in the custody of any office of the Supreme Court may be produced for use in another court (RSC, Ord 63, r 9). Application is made through the court having custody, and the documents are normally sent there by post (Supreme Court Documents (Production) Rules 1926).

Quarter sessions

Information available

The jurisdiction of courts of quarter session, abolished in 1971, was not only judicial but to some extent administrative. Their records often include copies of enclosure awards and maps, particulars of corn rents, details of highways and footpaths both public and private, plans of developments by public utilities, and orders for diverting public rights of way. Some records arising from the courts' judicial functions are not opened to public inspection for at least 30 years.

Details of some of the information available are given in *Quarter Sessions Records for Family Historians* by JSW Gibson (Federation of Family History Societies).

To whom available

Anyone may search.

How obtained

The records are normally lodged in the appropriate county record office, where personal application should be made. Requests for information not yet generally available should be made to the appropriate officer of the local Crown Court.

Cost

A search is normally free. A charge is made for copies.

Magistrates' courts

Information available

The court registers of magistrates' courts, including juvenile courts, contain details of convictions and sentences imposed.

To whom available

The registers are not open for public inspection for at least 30 years. The convicted person and his solicitor may apply for copies.

How obtained

A request should first be made to the clerk to the justices, who may refer the enquiry to the county record office if that is where the records are housed. The registers are not indexed, so full details—location of court and date of hearing—are needed to identify an entry.

Cost

A fee is charged for a certified copy entry.

Local authorities

Certain Acts, principally the Local Government (Access to Information) Act 1985, have made much of the meetings, reports, etc of local authorities available to the public. In this context (save where specifically stated otherwise, below) authority includes a joint authority, the Common Council, and combined police authorities that are bodies corporate and combined fire authorities.

Information available

A register must be maintained, containing the following information: the name and address of every member of the council and the ward/division he or she represents (for police, the appointing body); name and address of every member of a committee or subcommittee; a list of powers delegated to an officer of the authority and the title of the officer able to exercise the powers; and a summary of the public's rights to attend meetings and inspect documents.

Meetings are open to the public except to the extent that confidential information (defined broadly as information provided by a government department on terms forbidding its disclosure to the public, or whose disclosure is prohibited by statute or court order) or exempt information (this is defined in a Schedule to the Act and covers information relating to particular employees, former employees or applicants, recipients of services or assistance, information that would be regarded as legally privileged, identity of informants, etc) would be disclosed. Three days' notice must be given (less if convened at shorter notice) and once admitted the public cannot be excluded.

Agendas are open to inspection as are reports prepared for the meeting. Again, matters likely to arise where the public are excluded from the meeting are not covered. Inspection time limits are similar to those for calling meetings, and items may not generally be considered at the meeting unless the inspection provisions have been implemented.

Minutes and reports are available after the meeting, subject to similar exclusions. Similar provisions apply to background papers, but these need not be made available four years after the meeting in question. These provisions apply equally to committees and subcommittees.

To whom available

Anyone may inspect.

How obtained

By personal attendance at the offices of the authority in question. Other than for the major items listed above (agendas, minutes, etc), it is advisable to telephone first to ensure immediate availability.

Cost

Inspection, free of charge. A charge may be made for copies.

Accounts

Information available

The full accounts of any local authority and certain other public authorities with local responsibilities, and any auditor's report on them, are open for inspection by any local government elector for the area. He is also entitled to copies.

How obtained

Personal application should be made to the offices of the authority concerned.

Cost

Inspection, free. A reasonable fee may be charged for copies.

Records

Information available

Any map, plan or document deposited with the clerk to a local authority or chairman of a parish or community council or parish meeting, pursuant to the standing orders of either House of Parliament or any Act or statutory order, is open for inspection in the absence of a contrary provision in the instrument authorising its deposit. Copies may be made.

To whom available

Anyone may inspect.

How obtained

Application should be made in person to the offices of the authority concerned.

Cost

Inspection fee, 10p per hour.

Admissibility in evidence

A photographic copy of a document in the custody of a local authority or parish meeting is admissible in evidence to the same extent as the original, provided, if the original is in colour and that is relevant to the interpretation of the document, the copy distinguishes between the colours (Local Government Act 1972, s 229).

Generally

Information available

Comprehensive information about local authorities—elected members, principal officers, addresses of offices for different services, finance, etc—is given in *The Public Authorities Directory* (LGC Communications).

Lotteries

Information available

Returns relating to small lotteries promoted by societies established for charitable, sporting, cultural or other non-profit making purposes are available for inspection. They show the amount of the whole proceeds of the lottery, the amounts appropriated for expenses and prizes, and the amount applied to the purposes of the lottery, specifying those purposes. The dates between which tickets were sold are also given. The information is kept for at least eighteen months from the date of the return, which must be made within about three months from the draw.

To whom available

Anyone may inspect the returns.

How obtained

Application should be made in person to the offices of the London borough, borough or district council within whose area the head office of the society promoting the lottery is situated.

Cost

There is no fee.

Newspaper back issues

British Library

Information available

The most comprehensive collection of back issues of newspapers is held by the British Library. Its Newspaper Library contains London newspapers and journals from 1801 onwards, English provincial, Scottish and Irish newspapers from about 1700 onwards and large collections of Commonwealth and foreign newspapers. The Reference Division of the British Library holds London newspapers published before 1801, the London, Edinburgh, Belfast and Dublin Gazettes, additional files of *The Times*, *The Times Literary Supplement* and the *Illustrated London News* (1844–1892), and newspapers in oriental languages. UK newspapers have to be bound before they can be consulted, which means that there is a delay between publication and their being available, which may be as much as three years.

To whom available

Anyone over 21 may search after obtaining a reader's pass. Separate passes are required for the Colindale and Bloomsbury departments.

How obtained

To inspect newspapers, enquirers must attend personally, but copies may be ordered either personally or by post. The Newspaper Library is at:

Colindale Avenue, London NW9 5HE (Tel: 071–323 7353).

The search room is open Monday–Saturday 10 am to 4.45 pm, last orders taken at 4 pm.

The Reference Division is at:

Great Russell Street, London WC1B 3DG (Tel: 071–636 1544).

Cost

Searches, free. There is a wide variety of types of copy available from the Newspaper Library: photostats, black and white and colour photographs, transparencies and microfilms. Prices obviously vary both with the type of reproduction and the size of the copy. As a general guide, for personal callers copies are 60p to £1.23 a page depending on the source; by post, £10 for the first four pages, thereafter per personal callers.

Other libraries

Many principal libraries throughout the UK maintain collections of newspapers as do university libraries and the like. These are the best places at which to inspect back numbers. A selection of such libraries, often principally or exclusively local publications, is:

Belfast Belfast Education Library Board, Central Library, Royal Avenue, Belfast (Tel: 0232 243233).

Dublin National Library, Pearse Street, Dublin 2 (Tel: 010 353 1 777662).

Glasgow Mitchell Library, North Street, Glasgow (Tel: 041–221 7030)

Leeds Leeds Reference Library, The Headrow, Leeds (Tel: 0532 478274).

Liverpool William Brown Street Library, Liverpool L3 8EW (Tel: 051–225 5417).

Manchester Social Sciences Department, Central Library, Manchester M2 5PD (Tel: 061–234 1983/4).

Oxford Bodleian Library, Oxford OX1 3BG (Tel: 0865 277000).

Newspapers themselves

Most newspapers keep back issues, but for only a short time and often only for purchase (in person or by post), not inspection. Generally, when an issue is sold out it will not be reprinted. A selection of newspapers, with brief details, as follows.

Belfast Telegraph Circulation Dept Subscriptions Section, 124–132 Royal Avenue, Belfast BT1 1EB (Tel: 0232 224800). Six months' issues are kept, and the most recent three months' can be inspected. Copies may be purchased for the cover price.

Daily Mail Hart Mailing, 18 Hillside Avenue, Purley, Surrey CR8 2DP (Tel: 081–763 0140). Copies from 1988 onward are available, for purchase in person or by post. Cost varies with age, from £1 to £3.50 a copy.

Daily Telegraph Elkins Storage, 17 Orion Court, Cranes Farm Road, Basildon, Essex SS14 3DB (Tel: 0268 524285). Five years' back issues are kept until they run out (some go back ten years). They are available for purchase only, in person or by post (a telephone call to check whether the issue required is still available is recommended). Cost varies with age, from £1.38 to £5.50 a copy.

Dublin Independent Subscription Department, Independent Newspapers, Dublin 1 (Tel: 010 353 1 731666). Six months' issues are kept (unless sold out). Available for sale at 80p per copy for personal callers, £1.03 by post.

Financial Times 1 Southwark Bridge, London SE1 9HL (Tel: 071–873 4211). Twelve months' issues are kept, available for sale only, in person or through the post, at £1.60 per copy.

Glasgow Herald Circulation Department, 195 Albion Street, Glasgow G1 1QP (Tel: 041–552 6255). 12 months' back issues are kept. These may be purchased at the cover price, or 89p a copy by post.

Guardian Circulation Department, 119 Farringdon Road, London EC1R 3ER (Tel: 071–278 2332). Three months' back issues are kept. These may be purchased in person at the cover price or through the post from 164 Deansgate, Manchester M60 2RR at £1.10 per copy. There is also a service to supply a photocopy of any individual article (regardless of date) at £1.50 per article. The newspaper's library should be contacted.

Independent Readers Services, 40 City Road, London EC1Y 2DB (Tel: 071-253 1222). Back issues are available by post only. Approximately 12 months' are kept, but some older ones may be available. Cost per copy is £2 for the most recent month, £5 for those one to 12 months old, and £10 for those older than a year. There is an article copying service, also available by post only, at £1 a page.

Irish Times PO Box 74, 11-15 D'Olier Street, Dublin 2 (Tel: 010 353 1 792022). Roughly two months' back issues are kept. These may be inspected at the offices or will be supplied by post at £1.20 a copy.

Liverpool Daily Post and Echo Back Dates Department, PO Box 48, Old Hall Street, Liverpool L69 2EB (Tel: 051-227 2000). Two years' copies are kept and may be inspected. Those for approximately the last seven weeks may be purchased at the cover price.

Manchester Evening News Subscription Department, 164 Deansgate, Manchester M60 2RD (Tel: 061-832 7000). 12 months' issues are in stock. The most recent months are available for inspection; all may be purchased at cover price.

Observer Back Copies Department, Chelsea Bridge House, Queenstown Road, London SW8 4NN (Tel: 071-627 0700). Approximately four years' issues are available. These may be purchased at a price, varying with age, of 90p to £1.20 in person, £1.50-1.80 by post.

Sunday Telegraph see *Daily Telegraph*.

Sunday Times see *The Times*.

The Times Approximately six months' issues are kept, which may be purchased, in person or by post, at the cover price (plus postage). Personal callers should go to Ensign Centre, 28 Ensign Street, London E1 8ND; postal applicants write to News International, Back Dates, 1 Virginia Street, London E1 9BD (Tel: 071-782 5000).

Wales on Sunday Back Dates Circulation Department,

Thomson House, Havelock Street, Cardiff CF1 1WR (Tel: 0222 223333). One months' issues are kept and available for inspection; approximately a further two weeks' can be purchased. Cost, by post, £1 a copy.

Western Mail and Echo   see *Wales on Sunday* (save that cost is 65p).

Yorkshire Post   Back Copies Department, PO Box 168, Wellington Street, Leeds LS1 1RF (Tel: 0532 432701). Three months' copies are available to look at or to purchase (up to six months' may be). The cost is 78p a copy plus postage if mailed.

Index to the *London Gazette*

Information available

The index to the *London Gazette* is published annually in four volumes each covering one quarter. Arranged alphabetically, it lists individually references to the various notices on legal matters (eg bankruptcy, changes of name) published during the period covered. Company information published under EEC regulations is available on microfiche and may be consulted by personal callers.

To whom available

Anyone may consult the index.

How obtained

The index may be searched in person at the offices of the *London Gazette*:

51 Nine Elms Lane, London SW8 5DR (Tel: 071–873 8300).

Copies of the index are kept at most principal reference libraries and some main libraries. In London, in particular, at:

Guildhall Library, Aldermanbury, London EC2P 2EJ (Tel: 071–260 1868).

Here the index may be inspected personally and copies taken at a small charge. In addition, the Library offers a service to provide, through the post, a copy of a specific item or page, provided the information supplied by the searcher is sufficiently comprehensive for the item/page to be identified readily.

Cost

No charge for inspection.

Noise

Information available

An official noise measurements and particulars of noise reduction notices in a noise abatement zone must be registered by the local authority for the area.

To whom available

Anyone may search.

How obtained

Application should be made to the principal office of the authority concerned.

Cost

Search, no fee. Copies available at reasonable charge.

Electricity

Information available

Details of all licences granted under the Electricity Act 1989, including name and address of licensee, type of licence, licence number, issue and expiry dates and all associated documents. Also, all determinations and other related documents, including title of document, number and date of issue, and the licence to which it relates.

To whom available

Anyone may search.

How obtained

Application may be made in person or by post, to:

Office of Electricity Regulation (OFFER), Library and Information Centre, Hagley House, Hagley Road, Birmingham B16 8QG (Tel: 021–456 6377). Monday–Friday 10 am to 4 pm.

Cost

No charge for search. Copies: photocopies (subject to copyright), 10p a page plus VAT.

Gas

Information available

Details of licences granted to organisations to supply gas to the public and any revocation or modification thereof.

To whom available

Anyone may search.

How obtained

Application may be made in person (subject to a prior appointment) or by post to:

The Library, Office of Gas Supply (OFGAS), Stockley House, 130 Wilton Road, London SW1V 1LQ (Tel: 071–828 0898). Monday–Friday, 10 am to 4 pm.

Cost

No charge for search. Copies: £1 for the first five copies, 10p a page thereafter.

Telecommunications

Information available

Full details of all approved contractors and apparatus, and of all licences granted to public telecommunications operators.

To whom available

Anyone may search.

How obtained

Apply in person (having made an appointment) to:

Oftel, Export House, 50 Ludgate Hill, London EC4M 7JJ (Tel: 071–634 8700). Monday–Thursday 9.45 am to 5.15 pm (4.45 pm Friday).

Cost

Search, no charge. Copies may be made provided there are no copyright illustrations, at a cost of 10p plus VAT per copy.

Appendix

County Record Offices

Avon
Avon House, The Haymarket, Bristol BS99 7DE (Tel: 0272 290777).
Bristol City, The Council House, College Green, Bristol BS1 5TR (Tel: 0272 225692).

Bedfordshire
County Hall, Bedford MK42 9AP (Tel: 0234 363222).

Berkshire
Shire Hall, Shinfield Park, Reading RG2 9XD (Tel: 0734 233182).

Buckinghamshire
County Hall, Walton Street, Aylesbury HP20 1UA (Tel: 0296 395000).

Cambridgeshire
Shire Hall, Castle Hill, Cambridge CB3 0AP (Tel: 0223 317281).
Grammar School Walk, Huntingdon PE18 6LF (Tel: 0480 425842).

Cheshire
Duke Street, Chester CH1 1RL (Tel: 0244 602424).

Cleveland
Exchange House, 6 Marton Road, Middlesbrough TS1 1DB (Tel: 0642 248321).

Clwyd
46 Clwyd Street, Ruthin, Clwyd LL15 1HP (Tel: 0824 703077).

Cornwall
County Hall, Truro TR1 3AY (Tel: 0872 74282).

Cumbria
The Castle, Carlisle CA3 8UR (Tel: 0228 26247).

Derbyshire
County Offices, Matlock DE4 3AG (Tel: 0629 580000).

Devon
East Devon, Castle Street, Exeter EX4 3PQ (Tel: 0392 384251).
West Devon, Unit 3 Clare Place, Coxside, Plymouth PL4 0JW (Tel: 0752 385940).

Dorset
Bridport Road, Dorchester DT1 1RP (Tel: 0305 250550).

Durham
County Hall, Durham DH1 5UL (Tel: 091–386 4411).

Dyfed
Ceredigion Record Office, Swyddfa-R Sir, Marine Terrace, Aberystwyth SY23 2DE (Tel: 0970 617581).
County Hall, Carmarthen SA31 1JP (Tel: 0267 233333).
The Castle, Haverford West, Dyfed SA61 2EF (Tel: 0437 763707).

East Sussex
The Maltings, Castle Precincts, Lewes BN7 1YT (Tel: 0273 481000).

Essex
County Hall, Chelmsford CM1 1LX (Tel: 0245 430067).
Stanwell House, Stanwell Street, Colchester CO2 7DL (Tel: 0206 572099).
Central Library, Victoria Avenue, Southend on Sea SS2 6EX (Tel: 0702 612621 extn 215).

Gloucestershire
Clarence Row, Alvin Street, Gloucester GL1 3DW (Tel: 0452 425295).
Shire Hall, Westgate Street, Gloucester GL1 5TT (Tel: 0452 425289).

Greater London
40 Northampton Road, London EC1R 0HB (Tel: 071–332 3820).

Greater Manchester
56 Marshall Street, New Cross, Manchester M4 5FU (Tel: 061–832 5284).

Gwent
County Hall, Cwmbran NP44 2XH (Tel: 0633 838838).

Gwynedd
Archives and Museum Service, Victoria Dock, Caernarfon LL55 1SH (Tel: 0286 679095).
Cae Penarlag, Dolgellau LL40 2YB (Tel: 0341 422341).
Shire Hall, Llangefni, Anglesey LL77 7TW (Tel: 0248 750262).

Hampshire
Sussex Street, Winchester SO23 8TH (Tel: 0962 846154).
Civic Centre, Southampton SO9 4XL (Tel: 0703 223855).
3 Museum Road, Portsmouth PO1 2LE (Tel: 0705 829765).

Hereford and Worcester
The Old Barracks, Harold Street, Hereford HR1 2QX (Tel: 0432 265441).
County Hall, Spetchley Road, Worcester WR5 2NP (Tel: 0905 763763 extn 6351).
St Helen's, Fish Street, Worcester WR1 2NH (Tel: 0905 765922).

Hertfordshire
County Hall, Hertford SG13 8DE (Tel: 0992 555105).

Humberside
County Hall, Beverley, North Humberside HU17 9BA (Tel: 0482 885007).
Hull City, 79 Lowgate, Hull HU1 2AA (Tel: 0482 595102).

Isle of Wight
26 Hillside, Newport PO30 2EB (Tel: 0983 823821).

Kent
County Hall, Maidstone ME14 1XH (Tel: 0622 671411).

Lancashire
Bow Lane, Preston PR1 8ND (Tel: 0772 54868).

Leicestershire
Long Street, Wigston Magna LE18 2AH (Tel: 0533 571080).

Lincolnshire
The Castle, Lincoln LN1 3AB (Tel: 0522 526204).

Merseyside
Central Libraries, William Brown Street, Liverpool L3 8EW (Tel: 051–225 5417).

Mid Glamorgan
County Hall, King Edward VIII Avenue, Cardiff CF1 3NE (Tel: 0222 820820).

Norfolk
Central Library, Norwich NR2 1NJ (Tel: 0603 761349).

North Yorkshire
County Hall, Northallerton DL7 8AD (Tel: 0609 777585).
York City Archive, Exhibition Square, York YO1 2EW (Tel: 0904 651533).

Northamptonshire
Wootton Hall Park, Northampton NN4 9BQ (Tel: 0604 762129).

Northumberland
Melton Park, North Gosforth, Newcastle upon Tyne NE3 5QX (Tel: 091–236 2680).

Nottinghamshire
County House, Castle Meadow Road, Nottingham NG2 1AG (Tel: 0602 504524).

Oxfordshire
County Hall, New Road, Oxford OX1 1ND (Tel: 0865 792422).

Powys
County Hall, Llandrindod Wells LD1 5LG (Tel: 0597 823711).

Shropshire
Shirehall, Abbey Foregate, Shrewsbury SY2 6ND (Tel: 0743 252852).

Somerset
Obridge Road, Taunton TA2 7PU (Tel: 0823 337600).

South Glamorgan
County Headquarters, Atlantic Wharf, Cardiff CF1 5UW (Tel: 0222 872000).

South Yorkshire
Sheffield Archives, 52 Shoreham Street, Sheffield S1 4SP (Tel: 0742 734756).

Staffordshire
County Buildings, Eastgate Street, Stafford ST16 2LZ (Tel: 0785 223121).

Suffolk
Gatacre Road, Ipswich IP1 2LQ (Tel: 0473 264541).
Bury St Edmunds Branch, 77 Rangate Street, Bury St Edmunds IP33 2AR (Tel: 0284 763141).

Surrey
County Hall, Penrhyn Road, Kingston upon Thames KT1 2DN (Tel: 081–541 8800).
Castle Arch, Guildford GU1 3SX (Tel: 0483 573942).

Tyne and Wear
Blandford House, Blandford Square, Newcastle upon Tyne NE1 4JA (Tel: 091–232 6789).

Warwickshire
Priory Park, Cape Road, Warwick CV34 4JS (Tel: 0926 412735).

West Glamorgan
County Hall, Swansea SA1 3SN (Tel: 0792 471111).

West Midlands
Birmingham Reference Library, Birmingham B3 3HQ (Tel: 021–235 4219).

West Sussex
County Hall, Chichester PO19 1RN (Tel: 0243 533911).

West Yorkshire
Registry of Deeds, Newstead Road, Wakefield WF1 2DE (Tel: 0924 295982).

Wiltshire
County Hall, Trowbridge BA14 8JG (Tel: 0225 753641).

Index

births, marriages and
deaths in, 2
medical records, 22
service records, 25

Scotland—
adoption certificates, 12
births, marriages and deaths,
5–6
companies, 90 *et seq.*
Service records, *see also* Army;
Royal Air Force; Royal
Navy Army, 24
Royal Air Force, 25–6
Royal Navy, 25
Sewers, 65–6
Ships, 82–3
Social security—
benefits, 22–3
medical records, 20–1
Societies, 105–6
building, 104–5
certified loan, 107
industrial and provident, 106–7
Society of Genealogists, 35
Solicitors, 109–10
Sports, 116–17
Still births—
register of, 2

Street works, 64–5
Subsidence—
brine, 73
coal mining, 72–3

Telecommunications, 139
Tin mining, 74–5
Tithe redemption annuity, 62–3
Title—
registration of, 47–50
Town and country planning—
advertisements, 75
noise, 137
planning permission, 75–6
tree preservation orders, 67–8
Trade effluent, 66
Trade marks, 83–4
Tree preservation orders, 67–8
Trees
conservation areas, in, 68
preservation orders, 67–8

War-time debtors, 45
Wards of court, 27–8
Water resources, 69
Wills—
living persons, 28–9
proved, 29

Yorkshire Deeds Registries, 55–7